The Resurrection of History

The Resurrection of History

History, Theology, and the Resurrection of Jesus

DAVID BRUCE

FOREWORD BY
BRIAN ARTHUR BROWN

WIPF & STOCK · Eugene, Oregon

THE RESURRECTION OF HISTORY
History, Theology, and the Resurrection of Jesus

Copyright © 2014 David Bruce. All rights reserved. Except for brief quotations in critical publications or reviews, no part of this book may be reproduced in any manner without prior written permission from the publisher. Write: Permissions. Wipf and Stock Publishers, 199 W. 8th Ave., Suite 3, Eugene, OR 97401.

Wipf and Stock
An Imprint of Wipf and Stock Publishers
199 W. 8th Ave., Suite 3
Eugene, OR 97401

www.wipfandstock.com

ISBN 13: 978-1-62564-651-4

Manufactured in the U.S.A. 08/08/2014

Contents

Foreword by Brian Arthur Brown | vii

Preface | ix

1 Introduction | 1
2 History Matters | 15
3 The History of History | 34
4 The Theology of History | 53
5 The Employment of History | 70
6 The Enjoyment of History | 92
7 The Resurrection of History Matters | 113

Bibliography | 141

Foreword

In *The Resurrection of History*, David Bruce digs deeper than most New Testament scholars want to go.

Instead of naively assuming that the New Testament accounts of the resurrection of Jesus are "telling the truth" on the one hand or are just a pack of fables on the other, Bruce asks us to slow down and first ask the question, "What does it mean to say *anything* is historical?" He even opens the door to questions about the nature of reality, appropriate in this age of God particles and "quantum theology."

But David Bruce maintains focus on the issue of history, a question that is actually more difficult to answer than you might think. Many throughout the centuries have tried to answer it, but Bruce deftly shows how "what we think it means for something to be historical" is wrapped up in our different understandings of God, the universe, and even the meaning of life.

Rather than throwing up his hands in futility, Bruce engages some of the best historical, philosophical, and theological minds of the previous century, believing that if we are to take Jesus seriously, and wrestle with the Church's claims that he rose from the dead, we have to get our twenty-first-century thoughts organized. Bruce isn't afraid to critically examine the twentieth-century ideas of Bultmann and Barth, Moltmann and von Balthasar, or Crossan and Wright and to move beyond them. The hardest thing to believe about Bruce's exploration is how easy he makes it for readers like you and me to follow centuries of discussion about the most serious—and most controversial—claim of Christianity, enabling us to "move on" ourselves in ways that are faithful in our time.

In the end, Bruce comes out squarely on the side of the long-standing tradition of the Church as something that can and should be embraced,

Foreword

but only after facing the challenges head on. He argues that if Christians in our day and age want to take their own faith seriously, they will have to come to grips with what the first Christians genuinely thought and said about the resurrection of Jesus, and then seriously wrestle with how we may embrace those claims as our own, should we choose to do so. In the end, Bruce is more interested in twenty-first-century Christians speaking about their faith with integrity than "proving" the resurrection of Jesus to some imaginary neutral observer.

As a Christian minister, I have used David's *Jesus 24/7* series in my congregations, delighted by his ability to communicate the most subtle of concepts in the simplest, clearest way possible. As the author and editor of the *Three Testaments* series, I have been able to count on Bruce to represent the broader Christian tradition of the interreligious context in a manner that is not only faithful to the teachings of the church, but at the same time respectful of the beliefs of others. Recent Jewish commentary (*The Resurrection of Jesus: A Jewish Perspective*, by Pinchas Lapide) and traditional Islamic writings (questioning the crucifixion but not necessarily the resurrection) provide their own oeuvres on the profundities addressed by David Bruce, appropriate to interfaith conversations of a mutually respectful nature, which is becoming a twenty-first-century hallmark.

Whether you are Protestant or Catholic, liberal or conservative, or even if you are from another religious tradition "looking in" on what Christians are saying, you will find yourself challenged to go deeper into your own values, your own assumptions, and your own personal faith by letting David Bruce guide you in pondering the pivotal Christian claim that "Jesus Christ is risen indeed."

Brian Arthur Brown

Contributing editor,
Three Testaments: Torah, Gospel and Quran

Preface

ABOUT TWENTY-FIVE YEARS AGO, during my basic ministry studies with the United Church of Canada in Toronto, I wrote a brief paper on the symbolism of the resurrection of Jesus. In that short essay I argued that deciding whether the resurrection of Jesus was a historical event or simply an image of perennial truth would affect its symbolic value. The only trouble was that I had no idea what I was talking about, beyond that bare intuition. Twenty-five years and two doctorates later, I might confidently say I have half a clue—if only half. I am, however, like a wee lad with five loaves and a couple of fish, happy to share what I have with you.

I began my career in pastoral ministry believing that Jesus' resurrection was little more than a motif of hope, even if you would never have known it from my overly cautious sermons. I did believe that Jesus' resurrection was a historical event (though not necessarily a bodily one), and that God had done something within human history, but I largely lacked the conceptual apparatus to make much of a case for that. In this regard, I seemed to be well in step with my mainline Protestant colleagues.

The old Latin proverb *lex orandi, lex credendi* has often been quoted, and in my case it bore out. As I continued to preach, I grew more skeptical of my own position on the resurrection. I was finally caught up one fateful afternoon in a new-members class for a congregation I was serving, in which my wife Janet had decided to take part. She openly admitted to those gathered (and yes, I have permission to tell the story!) that she didn't believe in the resurrection or even in life after death, but that she hoped to live on in the memory of our children. There was stunned silence in the group. I finally ventured out, again more cautiously than is my natural bent, and commented, "Easter must be a bummer for you." We all laughed—which

Preface

was the desired outcome, but Janet said that yes, she had always felt a little alienated by the language of Easter.

That class was a great turning point for me. I soon enrolled in a doctor of ministry program in a leading seminary in order to critically examine both the content and process of my parish teaching. The result was—to my surprise—an increasing commitment to the orthodoxy of the ancient church and the importance of catechesis, and the publication of *Jesus 24/7: A Short Course in Faith for the Questing Christian*.[1] In that resource, I reaffirmed, in mainline Protestant language, the classic doctrines of the Trinity, the incarnation, and yes, the bodily, historical resurrection of Jesus. It seems that I wasn't alone in my interest to revisit the roots of Christian faith; even in my very liberal tradition, my little book sold very well, and was followed by *Jesus 24/7 Youth!*, *Jesus 24/7 Guide to the Bible*, and *Jesus 24/7 Guide to Spiritual Growth*.

Having positioned myself as a teacher, however, I realized that I still had much to learn, and so I returned to the specific question of the resurrection of Jesus in a second set of doctoral studies, this time at the Toronto School of Theology of the University of Toronto. At the urging of my supervisor Michael Bourgeois, my mentor Harold Wells, and my instructor and often-muse Fr. Gilles Mongeau, I made a study of historiography and historical method, and examined the question of what it would mean to declare the resurrection of Jesus to be a historical event. The result was a thesis with the sleep-inducing title (as all dissertations seem to have), "The Theological Implications of Declaring the Resurrection of Jesus to Be Historical." In it I traced the dialectical relationship between shifting historiographical trends and academic theology, especially where it concerned the resurrection of Jesus.

Along the way I had also begun exploring classic Christian spirituality, at least in its Western form. I began praying the Liturgy of the Hours, sneaking off to attend Mass whenever possible. I took detailed, in-depth catechetical instruction from the late Fr. Terrence Walsh, SJ, while under the wise and gentle spiritual direction of Ignatius Feaver, OFM. It was a seven-year journey that ended with my leaving the United Church of Canada and being received into the Catholic Church in July of 2011. I took up rich and satisfying work with homeless and marginalized men at the Good Neighbours' Club in downtown Toronto while becoming increasingly involved in the day-to-day life of the Catholic Church as a layperson.

---

1 Toronto: United Church, 2008.

Preface

I still run retreats, lead small groups, publish articles here and there (most recently writing the "Introduction to the Gospels" in Brian Arthur Brown's *Three Testaments: Torah, Gospel, Quran*,[2] and in these efforts seek to share my handful of insights with fellow travellers on life's journey.

My gratitude goes out to my longsuffering wife Janet, my now-grown children Heather, Geoffrey, and Paul, my mentors at the Toronto School of Theology, the wonderful Friars and my fellow parishioners at the Conventual Franciscan Parish of Saint Bonaventure, and to my publisher for enabling me to connect with you.

---

2 Lanham, MD: Rowman & Littlefield, 2012.

1 Introduction

In *Batman: The Dark Knight Rises*, Batman is surprised to see that an old nemesis, Ra's al Ghul, has escaped from the "inescapable" prison that he had been exiled to and presumably died in. The caped crusader, with a hint of whimsy, asks him what he had been doing with himself lately, to which his arch enemy replies that he has been busy practicing his favorite hobby: "Resurrection."

There is no doubt that the term "resurrection" is often used in a colloquial, casual fashion without theological implications. Most loosely, it acts as a synonym for "resurgence," as when the career of a politician or an athlete gets back on track after some time on the sidelines. In the case of Batman's enemy, as with anyone who has experienced prolonged unemployment, it can mean a return to active duty. For others, it means the return of hope and optimism, or simply even normalcy after a devastating setback or assault on their person.

When it comes to how scholars and believers view the resurrection of Jesus, there are essentially two points of view, with many subtle variations. Both have become widely influential in our time among both Catholics and Protestants. One point of view depicts the resurrection of Jesus as an event that happens independently of the perception of the disciples, which is then interpreted and transmitted by them. The other point of view depicts the resurrection of Jesus as an event that happens principally within or among the hearts and minds of Jesus' disciples, and what they transmit is their interior experience translated into narrative form. Before we examine in subsequent chapters the theoretical and technical issues involved in asserting either of these positions to be plausible, we need to be reasonable and commit to listening to both points of view.

The Resurrection of History

THE ORTHODOX UNDERSTANDING OF THE RESURRECTION OF JESUS

For some, the label "orthodox" may mean Orthodox with a capital "O" in distinction with Western, Catholic Christianity; for others, "orthodox" may mean communally responsible, and therefore morally virtuous; for still others, "orthodox" may mean the highly technical, over-refined dogmatic view defended by a monolithic medieval institution against all who would dare to think for themselves. In this writing, all I mean by the label "orthodox" is the core understanding most commonly held by the majority of Christians through the last twenty centuries. I might have preferred to use the label "traditional," but that label has already been taken up by a particular form of history writing, as you will see below.

The orthodox understanding is that Jesus was raised from the dead in the way that the texts of the New Testament portray: several days after his crucifixion, Jesus rose bodily from the dead, emerging from his tomb more than a full day after his crucifixion, and appearing to his disciples on several separate occasions. The resurrection signaled, among other things, Jesus' victory over sin and evil, God's acceptance of Jesus' death as an offering on behalf of humanity, and the issuing of a new invitation to all to participate in the divine life. Despite the recent trend toward vilifying the ancient and medieval church for holding unwaveringly to orthodox formulae as a means of controlling the faithful, there are actually several sources of motivation for the church for having maintained and still maintaining the traditional view of the resurrection of Jesus as an objective historical event, all of them honorable and worthy of thoughtful consideration.

First, the orthodox understanding is anti-reductionistic, and empowers those who are wary or at least skeptical of the tendency of the reigning *intelligentsia* to believe they have the last word on reality. Science, for instance, though long in the ascendancy in the Western world, can never finally furnish us with answers to the most fundamental questions of existence and meaning. A recent case in point was the discovery of the Higgs Boson, the so-called God particle, whose presence explained why atomic material has mass. While not discounting the scientific importance of this finding, most philosophers and theologians seemed unimpressed with the finding that there is more "stuff" in the universe than previously thought, since the more fundamental questions are (1) why there is any stuff at all? and (2) what is the point of anything existing in the first place? To reduce the resurrection of Jesus to the impact of the disciples' collective memory of Jesus is merely to replace metaphysics with psychology and reduce the ultimately mysterious workings of God to the relatively known quantities of human behavior, and in this way participate in "the domestication of the transcendent."[1]

Second, the orthodox understanding asserts that our understanding of what *is* must in some respects precede our understanding of what we *ought* to do. The resurrection of Jesus is a great big "stone in the river," around which our fluid debates about ethics and social progress must flow, because it reveals something of God's enduring character and God's purposes for humankind. Construing the resurrection of Jesus purely in terms of a metaphor with ethical implications begs the question of whose ethics we are employing: the ethics of the rich, the ethics of the poor, the ethics of the powerful, or the ethics of the weak. Ethics without attention to the *givens* of reality, whether metaphysical or historical, lacks any enduring points of reference and winds up being only the expression of the social order of the day. What we *ought* to be about must be more than a matter of social convention; it must be grounded in our most fundamental understandings of reality. If we endorse the idea that ethics are merely the production of a given society, we will ultimately have to evaluate all impetus for social reform as accidental by-products of history rather than the disciplined application of reasoned judgment, a view which denigrates human rationality and freedom. Enduring values require metaphysical grounding if they are to be the standard against which a society is measured, or else they are simply the dressed-up expressions of self-interest of different social groupings. Just as experimentation without attention to scientific method is only an application of the experimenter's own prejudices, so ethical reasoning without recourse to an overarching worldview or metanarrative has no claim to universality. If the resurrection of Jesus is a historical event, it could be regarded as revealing of the God who brought it about, and that would give us insight into the very values of God. In fact many argue that the significance of the resurrection lies in its eschatological (*eschaton* is a Greek word referring to the ultimate goal of history) character, that is, of what it says about human destiny and therefore proper human values.

Third, the orthodox understanding affirms the value of the body. In the broader Christian tradition, and especially in the Catholic and Orthodox traditions where the Real Presence of Christ in the Eucharist is upheld, the incarnation of God is understood to demonstrate the fundamental

---

1. Placher, *Domestication of Transcendence*.

goodness of material reality, including that of the human body. Respect for bodily existence impels Christians to feed the hungry, to house the homeless, and to provide medical care. Respect for bodily existence raises questions about purely utilitarian calculations in beginning-of-life and end-of-life matters such as abortion and euthanasia. Affirming the resurrection of Jesus as a historical event in which Jesus was *re-embodied* is consistent with the affirmation of the dignity of all bodily existence, including the very young and the very old. It also speaks a word of hope to those who have been marginalized for some bodily characteristic, whether that be gender, skin-color, infirmity, or relative physical or mental disability: God will ultimately vindicate that human suffering which occurs in virtue of our embodied existence by granting the transformation of our bodies into a fully perfected state: the resurrection of Jesus is God's seal on that promise for all of us. The body-affirming understanding of the resurrection of Jesus directs Christian ethical reasoning toward a holistic view of the human person and respect for basic material needs.

Fourth, the orthodox understanding provides solid grounding for continued humility. The belief that God intervened in human history carries with it the implication that humankind is not so evolved as to beyond the need of divine help. It also implies that there are possibilities for human transformation that are yet beyond our imagination, and that we are not capable of engineering humanity into a utopian state. The affirmation of the resurrection of Jesus as an objective, historical reality also keeps the *death* of Jesus in human view: the very rejection of God's self-presentation in Jesus reminds us that we are always quite capable of rejecting God and God's will, and in need of God's gracious response to our incompleteness.

I offer these considerations not as compelling arguments, or even as a complete typology of reasons for affirming the resurrection of Jesus as a discrete historical event. These four motivations however might at least be indicative not only of the range of thinking among those who would uphold this view.

THE REVISIONIST VIEW OF THE RESURRECTION OF JESUS

For some, the label "revisionist" may mean intellectually unfounded and academically irresponsible; for others, "revisionist" may mean radically rethought so as to bring contemporary humanity in touch with the

Introduction

spiritual dynamism of the early church; for still others, "revisionist" may mean relegating theology to a role subservient to other disciplines, such as philosophy, science, or history. By "revisionist" I mean the sincere attempt to reinterpret the resurrection of Jesus in ways more intellectually and spiritually satisfying than the orthodox understanding. While it could be successfully argued that there are many possible revisionist understandings of the resurrection of Jesus, I will choose the one that I understand to be perennial and, in many Christian circles, currently ascendant.

For many down through the centuries, the "resurrection" of Jesus can be understood along the following lines. Jesus, the popular preacher of the immanence of God's reign, was arrested, vilified, and crucified, his influence seemingly extinguished by the jealousy of the religious leaders of his day and the mighty indifference of the secular government. However, in remembering his teachings, and recalling his willingness to live according to those teachings even if it meant his death, the life of Jesus continued to inspire his disciples to imitate their master: in their renewed dedication to live lives completely dedicated to the good news of God's justice and love, Jesus' influence was "resurrected," brought back to life among his faithful followers. In such a scheme, the proclamation that God has "raised" Jesus means essentially that God has "exalted" Jesus in the minds of his disciples, and made him "Lord" by allowing his memory to become a controlling influence on the life of their community.

First, the revisionist understanding takes away the emphasis on the metaphysical. Categories of thought and experience change from century to century, and from culture to culture. Sometimes categories change within a given culture within a single century, as happened in the West with the adoption of Darwin's theory of natural selection in the nineteenth century or Einstein's theory of special relativity in the twentieth. We can't be expected to live in the thought world of the first century, with a flat earth, heaven "above" and hell "below." We don't routinely cast out evil spirits anymore, but treat people for mental illness instead. We need to reinterpret the narrative accounts of Jesus' resurrection in contemporary terms. To ask contemporary Christians to learn the language of ancient metaphysics is too daunting a task, and to ask people to abandon the fruits of human progress and embrace an outmoded worldview is cruel and unworthy of consideration. For most of us, highly abstract theoretical considerations that we might broadly call "metaphysical" are not what we enjoy talking about, much less pretend to understand, so how can that be an element of the gospel that Jesus preached to the poor and the downtrodden?

Second, the revisionist understanding places the emphasis on the ethical. If Christians are to live as people of hope, the resurrection of Jesus is the centerpiece of a faith that says God never gives up on any of us, no matter how dismal or unfair our circumstances. As the Gospels depict, Jesus' life is the ultimate morality tale: even if the entire world is against you, stay true to God, and God will vindicate you and your efforts. Even if you do not live to see this vindication, the truth will win out eventually, and your life will be understood and esteemed for its value by those who come after you. Granted we would all love to experience our vindication in our own lifetime, but we are called to take up the invitation to live as courageously as Jesus did, offering ourselves for the ongoing life of the world, even if that means the ultimate sacrifice of never knowing how or when your contribution will be appreciated. Perhaps this is what was meant by "becoming as little children," and being able to "give no thought for tomorrow," but abandoning oneself to God's assessment of our worth. This take on the resurrection of Jesus is not for the faint-hearted, but calls for a robust, courageous and world-engaging faith.

Third, the revisionist understanding acknowledges that you are not your body. The "I" that I know is different from my body: I can in some respects overcome my body, using mind over matter. This is a philosophical position that might conceivably be welcomed by those who are disabled, disfigured, or for other reasons that have to do with the condition of their bodies are marginalized by society. This also resonates with seniors, many of whom have to come to terms with the weakening of their bodies and the resulting lack of endurance and agility, and may also resonate with persons who are or are on the road to being transgendered and/or in the process of sex-reassignment. It may also be cherished by certain self-improvement movements, who focus on the mastery of the body. Discerning the action of God in Christ might lead us to look beyond the obvious features of the incarnation such as Jesus' maleness, his Jewishness, his personal piety, and even his first-century worldview. These elements of Jesus' life aren't things we can aspire to, so the meaning of the life, death, and resurrection of Jesus must lie beyond these physical and temporal considerations in a system of insights that is truly universal.

Fourth, the revisionist understanding makes the resurrection of Jesus something we can discuss in terms of contemporary historical reasoning.

Introduction

In a post-Enlightenment world, we no longer believe in miracles, at least not in the sense of events that require supernatural intervention. When historians encounter tales of miracles in ancient or medieval texts, they rightly assume that they are products of imagination or ignorance, stemming from a lack of scientific understanding of how the world actually works. Impartial historians would do far better to interpret the death and "resurrection" of Jesus within what we know of the unalterable laws of biology, namely that dead people do not spontaneously reanimate. Any other position is a retreat from the advance of scientific knowledge, and represents a break with the fundamental dictum that truth is truth no matter where we find it. A symbolic or subjective renewal of appreciation of what Jesus taught and stood for would be in keeping with our contemporary worldviews, and be salvageable for the inspiration of humanity in the third millennium. The narratives of Jesus' death and resurrection don't record a single historical event, but rather they represent an enduring appreciation of what has always been true, that the ongoing power of life conquers the ongoing power of death over the course of cosmological history just as surely as hope conquers despair within the smaller parameters of human history.

CAN WE DISMISS THE QUESTION?

On the one hand, most discussion of key points of doctrine should probably be considered as sincere attempts to find new ways to express agreement with the historic Christian faith; rushing to judgment and pronouncing those who would challenge long-held beliefs as heretics or standing outside the circle of faith does nothing to encourage us to understand those who hold contrary opinions, and closes off conversation before it can even begin. On the other hand, it would seem strange to declare once and for all that *all* Christian beliefs are negotiable, and that there is no need on our part in the present to identify with the faith of the church as it existed in the first century, and that there is no "deposit of faith" to be treasured for all time. While someone might want to defend this position, it would require an extraordinarily thorough reconceptualization of religion, tradition, and community, not only for Christians but for our understanding of other religions as well. Not all advocates of this newer understanding of the resurrection of Jesus would claim this radical step is implied in what they affirm; in fact, many would claim that revisiting the resurrection of Jesus in the manner they are suggesting would help the church to reclaim the

The Resurrection of History

original dynamics of faith lost when the church committed to analyzing and concretizing its faith in the language of Greek metaphysics.

Sincere and thoughtful people do sometimes differ, and that has to be acknowledged and truly *owned* by those who want to think through the question of Jesus' resurrection with any measure of seriousness. It is important to note that both points of view take the question of what kind of event the resurrection of Jesus is to be a relevant question. If the resurrection of Jesus was a historical event like other historical events, it potentially has different implications than if that is not the case. The resurrection of Jesus is the perfect test-case for studying the intersection of theology and history.

Some might want to dismiss the question and claim that it doesn't matter whether or not the resurrection of Jesus was a historical event. It might be ventured that what really matters is that people *believed* that the resurrection of Jesus was a historical event, and that's all that really matters. Such an attempt to shelve the question has its own implications, however. It suggests that those who presented the resurrection of Jesus to the world as a historical event—at least by the time the Gospel narratives were written—were self-deceived or intellectually limited, which would have to cast doubt on the intelligibility of their representation of Jesus' vision and ministry. It also suggests that those who lived—and in many instances, sacrificed—their lives for the integrity of the church in subsequent centuries were misguided, and perhaps to a large extent distracted from the real existential and ethical issues at hand. It further suggests that theologians, clergy, and dedicated lay persons have wasted enormous time, energy, and resources presenting, explicating, and defending something inconsequential, possibly indicating a deep-seated pathology on the part of the entire Christian movement.

An analogy might be that of the original moon landing. Some conspiracy-theorists claim that the moon landing was faked, with footage of the "lunar" event actually shot in a television studio to spare the American government the embarrassment that they had failed in their promise to put a man on the moon and thereby demonstrate global technological supremacy. In some respects, it might be true that if the moon landing was faked, it had much the same consequences as a successful mission: the expansion of funding to the space program and the inspiration of the American people. In other respects, the consequences of pronouncing the original moon landing to have been faked are enormous in terms of what that says about the relationship of the American government to the American people, in

Introduction

terms of social spending priorities, and in terms of the positioning of the United States in the global community. Beyond the emotional distress of having "lived a lie," any American citizen has to consider the opportunity-cost of those funds going to the space program that might have gone to improving health and education or other social infrastructure, or the impact of an *unearned* reputation for America's role as technologically dominant on its self-appointed role in policing global conflicts.

Even if the consequences of misconstruing the resurrection of Jesus to be a historical event were not so dire, to take the position that the historical question doesn't matter is in effect to have already taken up the revisionist point of view. In saying that the question of whether or not the resurrection of Jesus was an historical event doesn't matter is to say that the *real* event was the psychological conversion of the disciples of Jesus to declare him as alive in their own faith and witness to his life and teaching.

WHAT THIS BOOK DISCUSSES

The question of the nature of the event of the resurrection of Jesus is not an easy one to discuss, as it involves questions of metaphysics, epistemology, systematic and pastoral theology, and the faith of real women and men all around the world. It shouldn't come as any surprise that the editorial comment that "the world itself could not contain the books that would be written" about Jesus (John 21:25) follows that Gospel's resurrection narratives. There has been an enormous amount of ink spilled over the subject of Jesus' resurrection, and what you are reading is just a little more.

Most of what has been written about the resurrection has been devotional and inspirational literature in which the question of whether or not the resurrection of Jesus was a historical event isn't raised, either because the authors hadn't thought much about these questions, or assumed (perhaps rightly) that this wasn't a question their readers were prepared to pursue. It may be safe to say that for most Christians through most centuries of the church's existence, the question of whether or not the resurrection of Jesus was a historical event was something only examined by professional theologians and more thoughtful clergy.

More recently, in the last couple of centuries, the question of whether or not the resurrection of Jesus was a historical event has reemerged among scholarly theologians in response to shifting worldviews. Many of these scholars ventured that the resurrection of Jesus was not a historical event, at least not in the sense that other chronicled events are considered historical, and were quite inventive in offering new categories of language, writing, and community tradition to help others grapple with their insights. Many of them tried to preserve the fundamental meaningfulness of the resurrection of Jesus as an element of Christian faith without committing themselves to declaring it to be a historical event, at least not along the lines of the traditional view. Other authors, especially among American evangelicals in the last century, offered vigorous defenses of the resurrection as a historical event, but often did so without much regard to either the profundity of their opponents' arguments or attention to the theoretical question of what makes *any* event a historical event. Some of those writings, despite their shortcomings, are encyclopedic in their amassing of details, and we owe them a debt of gratitude for their efforts to uncover the truth.

This book is unique (or at least very rare) in its focus on issues that should be examined before anyone plunges into weighing and judging the evidence on the resurrection of Jesus. Just as courts are guided by rules of law, historians are guided by certain methodological rules. However, just as the law evolves, slowly and carefully, so the rules of historical method evolve, slowly and carefully. There is no one body of historians who make up the rules that historians have to use when engaged in their craft, and there are differing opinions about the how to prioritize recognized elements of sound history writing. Most historians, I have discovered, don't regard themselves as experts on historical method, but tend to write the findings of their historical research in an intuitive fashion, along the lines of the kinds of history writing they have known and admired. Over the last couple of centuries there have been discernible shifts in thinking—at least in the Western world—affecting the work of the majority of professional historians, and some of what follows is an attempt to take those shifts into account when approaching the question of whether or not the resurrection of Jesus is an historical event. I will, in a way, argue that the discipline of history writing almost died and has been resurrected in a form that allows it consider the resurrection of Jesus on historical terms.

I will try to offer some background on the development of contemporary historical method and outline some of the shifts that have occurred, in increasing detail as we approach our own day, and discuss how they affect our central question. I will also trace how these shifts were confronted or embraced by some of the greater theological minds of the twentieth century. As the reader will see, I have chosen to dwell on the work of those theologians whose writings feature significant reflection on the issue of whether or not the resurrection of Jesus was historical. I will also engage the multidisciplinary world of New Testament scholars, who are implicitly historians *and* theologians. Along the way I will uphold the coherence of both the revisionist and traditional views of the resurrection of Jesus, but in the end I will affirm, for what I hope will be considered sound methodological reasons, the viability of the orthodox position. I will finish up by addressing in detail a few of the implications for Christian faith in the twenty-first century of declaring the resurrection of Jesus to be a historical event.

It is my casual, unscientific observation that evangelical Protestants in most parts of the world hold strictly to the orthodox understanding of the resurrection as a nonnegotiable, *sine qua non* of their faith, and are typically baffled as to how anyone claiming to be a Christian can seriously entertain any other point of view. I hope that evangelical Protestant readers will be able to bracket any discomfort they might have with my being Catholic and enjoy the convergence of evangelical Protestant and orthodox Catholic conclusions. I also observe that many mainline Protestant denominations are split between orthodox and revisionist understandings of the resurrection, with the vast majority of them not wishing to stir up troubles over what seems an obscure metaphysical issue when there are other urgent matters to attend to. I hope that mainline Protestant readers will consider the resurrection of Jesus central enough to their faith that they will see how their understanding of the resurrection of Jesus, their understanding of the mission of Jesus, and their understanding of the person of Jesus need to be woven together for the sake of their faith's integrity. And I also observe, with a great deal of intrigue, how relatively few Catholics in my orbit have thought through this issue, seemingly accepting the orthodox understanding—more or less. Catholics, it seems, have long lived in a world of one-offs, of historical singularities, and imagine the resurrection of Jesus to be just one more of these. I do hear, however, listening between the lines of homilies as I visit different parishes and hear different priests, the tendency to treat all questions of the historicity of the resurrection of Jesus, as if they are simply a mythological representation of saying that Christ is present to us in the Eucharist. I hope Catholics will appreciate my concern that this kind of "translation" of the resurrection of Jesus into Eucharistic theology may ultimately undermine the orthodox understanding of Eucharist as well as the resurrection.

HOW TO USE THIS BOOK

It may be my author's vanity, but I think I have written a book that can be used in different settings. Holding two earned doctorates, I may now have spent enough time inside university and seminary classrooms to know what kind of things students discuss at various levels and in various settings. I have also been in pastoral ministry for twenty-five years, so I think I have a fair notion of the kind of questions that are helpful in an adult study-group setting. I now work outside both academic and ecclesiastical settings, having been "returned to the wild" of the laity, and have become reacquainted with the kind of questions that everyday followers of Jesus wrestle with in times of prayer and reflection.

At the end of each chapter are three sets of questions.

The first set is labeled "Seminary" and is intended for senior undergraduates or basic degree seminary classes. Many of them could be assigned as study questions in lecture courses, but they are really intended for discussion. These questions tend to suspend any particular faith-commitment.

The second set is labeled "Study Group" and is intended for use among adults in typical Catholic parish and Protestant congregational settings. These questions presuppose that the participants are practicing Christians with some rudimentary understanding of the Christian tradition. Wrestling with these questions might be aided by the presence of a priest, minister, or educated lay-person, but the presence of such a resource person isn't presumed. Some groups who are without a resource person have found it helpful to note questions they found difficult and assign a group member to seek out someone outside the group who can be of assistance.

The third set is labeled "Individual" and is intended for personal reflection. The answers to these questions are likely to be of a nature that should only be shared with a close friend or a spiritual director, and are not normally intended for group discussion. If, however, two or more people who are very well-acquainted with each other are reading this book together, these questions might be considered in conversation. I only recommend that you decide beforehand if these questions will be part of your study-covenant: no one likes to be ambushed!

In all likelihood, most readers of this book will be flying solo. I understand the temptation to read a book like this like a novel, turning the pages as fast as one can, ignoring the chapter-ending questions as peripheral. I recommend, though, that you at least scan the questions at the end of each chapter, take a moment to consider your own thoughts, and mark any that

Introduction

you would like to return to someday when you have more time. When you are finished reading this book it would probably prove very helpful for you to flip through and take a second look at the questions you marked, and consider whether or not your reading and reflection have offered any further answers for you along the way.

And one more word. The research that stands behind this little book took me several years to conduct, and resulted in the writing of a thesis that I successfully defended for my PhD. You might not agree with my conclusions, but I can assure that the research is solid. I have, however, beefed up the theological conclusions now that I have a little more freedom to do so. For those of you who are only too glad this seems to be written by your local green grocer rather than someone who has spent too long in "the ivory tower," you're welcome.

The Resurrection of History

QUESTIONS FOR CONSIDERATION

Seminary

1. What authors are you familiar with who might hold the revisionist view or the traditional view of the resurrection of Jesus?
2. What do you already know about the elements of historical method?

Study Group

1. What parts of the revisionist and traditional views of the resurrection of Jesus appealed to you? Why?
2. How much does anyone have to *know* before they can be called a Christian?

Individual

1. When have you ever defended a position you didn't really believe in, and what was the result?
2. What elements of the Christian faith do you have secret doubts about?[

2 History Matters

DID HE OR DIDN'T HE? In this morning's paper the lead story here in Canada was about Jason Kenney, minister of immigration, who has been accused of personally intervening on behalf of convicted felon Conrad Black. Lord Black, you may recall, came to international fame by becoming the publisher of the *London Telegraph*, the *Chicago Sun-Times*, and the *Jerusalem Post*, as well hundreds of other newspapers across North America. For his part in rescuing the *Telegraph*, Mr. Black was awarded a British peerage, becoming the Right Honourable Lord Black of Crossharbour. The Canadian prime minister at the time, the Right Honourable Jean Chrétien, often a target of Black's media clout and conservative views, invoked an obscure Canadian law and demanded that Black renounce either his peerage or renounce his Canadian citizenship. Black was so outraged at this attempt to embarrass him among his fellow Lords that he renounced his Canadian citizenship, even though he and his Canadian wife continued to maintain a house in Toronto as one of their principal residences.

Several years later, embroiled in financial troubles, Black was charged and convicted in the United States of fraud and obstruction of justice, and sentenced to prison in Florida. After successful legal challenges to two of his three convictions, he served a total of three and a half years, and was released in May 2012. Since he was no longer a citizen of Canada, in anticipation of his release Black requested and received a temporary residence permit—a permit that would require renewal every year—to enter and live in Canada. As soon as he was released, he returned to Canada.

Noted immigration lawyer Guidy Mamann, in response to questions posed to him by the press, said he thought it was highly unlikely that someone of Black's status and circumstances would have been granted a temporary residence permit without the knowledge of the minister of immigration,

The Resurrection of History

Jason Kenney. By saying that Kenney, the immigration minister, knew of the application, he was clearly implying that Kenney personally influenced the decision, a process typically left for bureaucrats to impartially decide, interfering in what should be a straightforward, non-politicized process. Kenney denied the allegation, and one of his aides pursued the matter, asking the Law Society of Upper Canada to censure Mamann for bringing the minister of immigration into disrepute. The Law Society of Upper Canada rejected the complaint, so more recently a group of Canadian immigration lawyers, led by Lorne Waldman, wrote a letter to the minister of immigration agreeing with Mamann's contention that it was highly improbable that the decision to grant the residence permit to Black was made "without any input from yourself," further asserting that they found "the attempt by you and your officials to muzzle freedom of expression to be reprehensible."[1]

Kenney's office responded, saying, "We gave [Waldman] the opportunity to review documents that contradict his and Mr. Mamann's false accusations. Unfortunately, rather than review the evidence and pursue the truth as one would expect from a lawyer, he chose the path of shameless self-promotion and public spectacle." Kenney maintains that, after learning about Black's application for the permit in February, he turned the matter over to civil servants without further comment.

No doubt this story might seem like a very minor matter, but it could prove otherwise. Americans know from following presidential politics how major scandals start out in such minor events. There are a number of relevant background elements that come into play, which make the story more intriguing.

Since the time when Black was imprisoned, Jean Chrétien's Liberal Party, under a new leader, lost the federal election (and two more since) to Stephen Harper's Conservative Party, who have formed a government far more in step with Black's political and economic views. Black's largest Canadian newspaper, the *National Post*, is highly sympathetic to Harper's government. Furthermore, Harper's government has routinely been characterized as more secretive and less open with the press about its inner workings than previous governments, and this allegation plays right into that perception, something that isn't likely to be well received by the Canadian public. Still further, Prime Minister Harper has a reputation for being the most hands-on leader this country has had in decades, reading every file, scanning every brief, and having full control of his cabinet ministers.

---

1. *Globe and Mail*, August 2, 2012.

History Matters

If Kenney influenced the decision to grant a residence permit to Black, is it possible that Harper was kept in the dark, or did this decision go all the way to the top? And yet further, if this decision in Black's favor did come from the highest levels, and someone who is a friend of the government's and among the super-rich appears to receive preferential treatment, and those voicing concern over the truth or even the perception that this is the case are threatened with harm to their careers—in this case, disbarment—what does that say about the current government's values?

When the next election comes, a lot could rest on the answer to the question, "Did he or didn't he?" A lot rides on the facticity of one tiny purportedly historical incident, an incident that no one has stepped forward to testify to, an incident that is at this point only an inference based on probabilities that are themselves dependent on a set of observed behaviors. Simple or complex, history matters.

The judgment that something is in fact historical, that some report of an incident is in fact true, routinely determines whether or not someone keeps her job or is fired, whether someone gets to keep custody of his children or must relinquish that role to someone else, and in some jurisdictions whether or not someone lives or dies. Our entire system of justice is based on investigating whether or not alleged behavior actually took place. Documents, eyewitness testimony, expert opinions, and even previous rulings involving similar elements are all weighed in the minds of judges and jurors until a verdict—a fallible but highly consequential verdict—is delivered.

Even when past events occurred too long ago for us to question eyewitnesses, those events can and are routinely reconstructed in narrative form in order to provide perspective on present day realities. Let me offer an example.

My last name is Bruce. Everywhere I go, I get called "Bruce" as if that were my first name. I am used to that by now, but for years I'd wished I had a last name that was more commonly a surname, like Smith, Jones, or McDonald. And though I never asked them, I bet my children felt the same way—that is, until one summer when we went to Scotland on a family holiday. From Edinburgh we took a bus out to Stirling, and toured the museum situated at the historical site of the Battle of Bannockburn, which tells the story of the rise of Robert the Bruce as king of Scotland, and Bruce's decisive victory over superior English numbers in June of 1314 that paved the way for centuries of Scottish independence. Just as awe-inspiring as the statue of a mounted Bruce at Bannockburn was the image of our great

The Resurrection of History

ancestor carved into a pillar of the main gate of Stirling Castle. Bearing the surname of that great warrior made our hearts swell with Scottish pride, and we couldn't help but wonder if bearing the surname Bruce didn't entail some kind of obligation to embody his virtues: his courage, his cunning, his determination. At some point during the day, my son turned to me and said, "Now I understand what it means to be a Bruce."

Ask anyone why they feel it is important to be Italian, Kenyan, or Australian, and once they've told you what they treasure about their national identity, they will usually be happy to relate a culturally authorized and highly polished historical narrative, one that involves a battle, a migration, a flourishing kingdom, the rise of a great hero, or the invention of some great contribution to civilization.

For those of us who are Christian, we likely carry with us a small batch of stories that we trot out to explain why we identify with the particular branch of the church we find ourselves in. Christians from India proudly relate the tradition that the Apostle Thomas travelled to India and founded congregations there. Roman Catholics talk about the crucifixion of St. Peter in Rome. Lutherans and Anglicans share the stories of Luther and Cranmer (and maybe even Henry VIII), and Methodists recall the tireless work of the Wesleys. In cases like these, historical events aren't simply curiosities, the answers to the Sunday *Times* crossword, but serve as vital, genetic components of our identities, and help explain why we are the way we are, as if they had a force that reached far into their own future. History matters.

A few weeks ago I had the pleasure of the company of one of my favorite theological discussion partners, a rabbi of the Reformed tradition of Judaism. She asked me about this project, and she offered, in revisionist fashion, the opinion that it didn't really matter to her whether or not so many million Jews left captivity in Egypt or not. I then asked her about the law. Allowing for her view that the law had been collected and edited over centuries rather than dictated to Moses quite as literally as is portrayed in the Pentateuch, I asked her whether or not it mattered that the law was *given* by God, rather than being a purely human construction. She agreed that it mattered a great deal, and I pressed on, asking her whether or not the scholarly pursuit of when and where certain elements of the law (e.g., the Ten Commandments, the sacrificial laws, Moses' farewell address) came into being was of any value, and she said yes, it mattered very much. When I asked her if she was prepared to agree with me after all that history does matter, she hesitated, so I went for the jugular. I asked her if it matters whether or not the Jewish people exist. She laughed out loud and said that *of course* it matters. And does it matter, I playfully demanded, that the Jewish people be understood in historical terms? We both smiled broadly as it was *her* turn to say, "Okay. History *matters*."

I would go so far as to say that history matters to each and every one of us each and every day. I get up in the morning and after breakfast walk to a certain street corner to catch a bus to work. Why do I stand there, and not somewhere else? Because I remember having caught the bus there on previous occasions. Why do I take that bus to a certain destination, and enter a certain building, expecting to be recognized? Because I remember having done so before. We have all seen movies where someone experiences partial or total amnesia (we may have even encountered it directly ourselves or in someone close to us), and we realize just how much of who we are and what we do is dependent on accurate memory of past events. Even on an individual, personal level, history matters—it matters very much.

WHAT IS "HISTORY"?

History is the past that matters in the present.

Quantum mechanics and parallel universes aside, philosophers and historians tend to agree that there is such a thing, in this time-line at least, as "the past." The past is the collection of all mental, verbal, and physical events that have occurred prior to the present. These events all took place in the context of other events, shaping and being shaped by those other events. These events were all in principle observable or relatable by those present at the time, even if a *complete* description of these events can never, in practice, be reconstructed, because no one has the time or ability—even if they had the inclination—to sort out every possible point of view on any given event. Declaring the past to be real is the same sort of fundamentally metaphysical decision as declaring the world to be real: you may have your doubts, but if you don't suspend those doubts you won't find many people willing to talk to you for very long.

"History" is a subset of the past. The existence of "history" is based on a process of selecting, consciously or unconsciously, some events as being highly significant for our appreciation of the present. This selecting is naturally relative to the interests of whoever is doing the selecting. For the most part, because of their relative power to influence economies, armies, and culture, much of what we call "history" has to do with royalty, military commanders, great thinkers, and artists. It is actually mind-boggling to recognize how *few* people, places, and events of the past have been considered material for the subject of history, whether that history consists of the known chronology of the local cider mill or the collection of widely known facts that might appear on a television game show. History is in fact a miniscule sliver of the past.

In English, there are several more terms that further refine our understanding, all of which are variations on the word "history." The first is "historical," which is used to indicate that a purported event did in fact happen—or at least is determined to have happened by the majority of those employing recognized standards of *historical writing* or *historical method* (something that I will discuss at length in this book). It's as if a verdict has been handed down, and some hypothesis, some educated conjecture, of what has happened in the past has been confirmed: that judgment is usually referred to as an event's *historicity*. If an event's historicity is accepted, it can be referred to as a *historical fact*, meaning that it has been deemed—at least by those involved in the conversation—worthy of being relied on in the attempt to reconstruct what happened in a particular case. Further research, of course, can cast doubt on the historicity of something once thought of as a historical fact: its historicity can be revoked, and it would no longer be eligible to be used as evidence in a historical reconstruction, unless it was flagged as doubtful.

The art of history writing is the art of discovery. Like a detective trying to solve a crime, a historian looks at the evidence at hand, does a little digging to see if there are any more reliable pieces of evidence that might have been previously overlooked, and then creates a *hypothesis*, a tentative reconstruction, of what happened. The best history writing attempts to take the most solid evidence available, including the reconstructions created by other historians, ask some hard questions about why any of the facts at hand were included, excluded, or thought to be of greater or lesser significance, then adopt a new or adjusted perspective, and finally create a new hypothesis and express it in narrative form. In the case of Mr. Kenney, the allegation that he influenced the bureaucratic process regarding Black's temporary resident permit is a *historical fact*: it is well documented and now part of the public record. However, the *hypothesis* that he actually did anything to influence that process has not yet been proven, at least in the minds of most observers, at least not beyond all reasonable doubt. Without a "smoking gun"—that is, hard evidence that would confirm the allegation was justly made, such as a memo or an email or even the unambiguous and disinterested testimony of the bureaucrat who signed the permit—Kenney's exertion of influence should not be regarded as a proper historical conclusion; most historians would see this as a violation of sound *historical method* and therefore poor *history writing*. Any history writing, any narrative that assumed Kenney's guilt would be flawed to the extent that it relied on this unproven hypothesis.

Another term we need to keep in view is "historic." Of the many things in the past that could be regarded as historical, some are more clearly seen to have wide-ranging implications for the way that we interpret the present, and these are often referred to as *historic*. Historic figures and events are seen as generating history. By way of example, many minor royal figures in Europe died in the first half of the twentieth century—their deaths are historical facts, which are recorded, searchable, and verifiable—but few are cited as frequently as the assassination of the Archduke Ferdinand, whose death set off a chain-reaction of political and military consequences that resulted in the onset of WWI. His death—perhaps more important than the accomplishments of his life—was not only historical but *historic*. In the case of Mr. Kenney, the controversy over his alleged use of ministerial power may in fact just fade away, dying a natural death for lack of evidence, or being overshadowed by larger events. His use of influence could prove to be historical, and not historic; on the other hand, if it is widely believed that Kenney acted as he denies, if "perception becomes reality," the controversy could prove to be historic without their being any historical fact at the heart of it—such is political life!

It should be quite clear that what is considered historical by one generation might be declared as unhistorical by another. For instance, the historical verdict of the Warren Commission that Lee Harvey Oswald acted alone in shooting President Kennedy may one day be modified or overturned; less consequentially, an aging Elvis might be discovered eating fried chicken at a roadside diner in Mobile, Alabama, in which case the historical record of his death would have to be expunged. Sometimes the very same data, when viewed through a different lens with modified assumptions, can yield strikingly different results. In this respect historical research can be seen as analogous to medical research: studies using certain assumptions and certain methods yield certain results, but then the *implications* of the results are subject to interpretation and debate. To write off historical research as merely subjective, however, would be to go too far, just as ignoring the contribution of medical research because of its occasional ambiguity would be to throw the baby out with the bathwater. In the same way that a scientist's revisiting of the relationship between pesticides and cancer rates could prove worthwhile in calling for the elimination of certain carcinogenic chemicals, a historian's revisiting of accepted historical reconstructions of, for instance, the relationship of Caucasians and aboriginal populations might prove worthwhile in creating a fairer resolution of existing disputes and land-claims.

And yet another verbal variation to watch for (English is a subtle and confusing language) concerns the use of the word "history" itself. Most of the time we use the word history to refer to, as I said above, those past events that are seen to have significance for the present. Sometimes, however, we use the word "history" to refer to *the work of historians*, since what historians produce is the narrative reconstruction of history: the craft is named after the product. If that seems a little abstract, consider the word "plumbing": it refers both to the craft of being a plumber—the knowledge, skills, and ability required to be a plumber and to work on pipes—and to the object of the plumber's craft: the pipes, pumps, and valves through which water flows are often referred to collectively as "plumbing," as in "The plumbing in that house is brand new." Where possible, I have tried to remember to use the term "historical research" or "historical inquiry" rather than just "history" to signal this usage, but there may be times that I have used the pairing of "theology and history" to indicate the academic disciplines involved. There are also times when you will see the word "historiography," usually when I am quoting someone else. When properly used, this term refers to history writing, the principles of weighing evidence in history writing, and the history writing of a particular time and place, such as "Ancient Chinese historiography." I have avoided using this term as much as possible, knowing that this book may well be the first that many will be reading on the subject of history writing, and I hated to pack too much into a single word if I could avoid it.

Finally, while lots of casual observers have opinions on various historical subjects, those who dedicate significant time and resources to such subjects are those that are usually referred to as "historians." Historians, like "journalists" or "scientists," come in all shapes and sizes. Some are mainstream academics, and recognized by having articles appear in respected, peer-reviewed publications, while others are relative amateurs, who pursue historical investigations with all the passion of a hobbyist. All historians work within the parameters of their own worldviews, but worldviews are never totally fixed, and I should declare my admiration for those historians who are willing to leave their worldviews open to modification based on the results of historical investigations—their own or those of others.

WHAT IS "RESURRECTION"?

"Resurrection" is a term packed with theological meaning, and a great deal of what follows in subsequent chapters has to do with unpacking that meaning, in light of what historians can and cannot do within the scope of their historical investigations. At this point, it is important to establish that the Christian tradition sets forth a particular historical claim regarding the historical figure of Jesus of Nazareth, using the term "resurrection." To understand this claim—suspending, for the moment, any judgment on whether or not we should deem this purported occurrence to be historical in the sense of having in fact happened—we should explore what Christians have meant by "resurrection."

It is vital to remember that Jesus was Jewish, his inner circle was Jewish, and before his death and for several years afterwards virtually all of his followers were Jewish. While Jewish thinking at the time of Jesus was not monolithic, the centrality of the reading and interpretation of their scriptures for their religious life is unquestionable. While temple life and sacrificial worship were important in Jerusalem and surrounding areas, the vast majority of Jews lived dispersed throughout the Roman Empire, largely out of touch with the temple and its priesthood. Rather, it was the weekly reading and interpretation of the scriptures in the life of the local synagogue developed centuries before during the Babylonian captivity (a practice Jesus himself regularly participated in) that bound Jews together in their religious and ethnic identity. The Sadducees ruled the temple priesthood, and there were various movements of political revolution (known as Zealots) or communal isolation (e.g., the Essenes), but the vast majority of Jews in Jesus' day were influenced by the Pharisaic movement, who excelled in scriptural interpretation and its ethical implications. The Pharisees regarded the collection of ancient psalms and the writings of certain prophetic figures as sacred scripture alongside the *Torah*, the law of Moses. This was the tradition that Jesus participated in when, in his hometown of Nazareth, he read from the scroll of the prophet Isaiah (Luke 4:16–30). This was also the tradition that the highly influential Saul of Tarsus / Apostle

Paul was trained in, something that he boasted about rather than concealed (Phil 3:5).

The Pharisees firmly believed in the resurrection, an idea that had gradually evolved in Hebrew/Jewish theology. According to Jewish prophets, priests, and poets, God had proved to be a God of justice, as demonstrated above all in providing for their exodus from slavery in Egypt, and in giving them the law through Moses as a means by which they might live in just relationships among themselves. As a tiny nation among more powerful neighbors, their belief in God's merciful justice served as the explanation of their fortune, both in good times and in bad: when times were bad, they got what they deserved, but God's covenantal love for them meant that God would always provide opportunities for repentance, and a restoration of the relationship of the nation with God. As their understanding of God expanded beyond that of a partial, tribal deity to a cosmic creator, God was seen to be not only the God of the nation but of heaven and earth. Their understanding of God's merciful justice became universalized and was converted into a metaphysical concept: not only would God rescue their national existence from its "death" at the hands of more powerful nations (Isa 26, Ezek 37), but each individual life would stand to be redeemed from the grave at the end of time, to receive the rewards and punishment dictated by divine justice (Dan 12).

The emergence of this concept might have been partly due to a gradual acceptance of Plato's ideas about the distinction of body and soul. While Roman military might dominated the Western world, including the Holy Land, for the century and a half before the birth of Jesus, Greek philosophy in its various forms served as the common intellectual touchstones among the educated. With several centuries of growing influence, it is probable that popular versions of Greek philosophy were accessible to most people in first-century Palestine. The Platonic distinction of body and soul, with the body being regarded as corruptible and dispensable and the soul being regarded as eternal and indispensable, fed a growing individualism: one might belong to a nation or a people by virtue of one's bodily existence, but a person should be essentially identified with his or her soul, whose fate was ultimately beyond all earthly attachments. In some ways this thinking was an extension of the sensibilities of the exilic and post-exilic Hebrew prophets: "The person who sins shall die. A child shall not suffer for the iniquity of a parent, nor a parent suffer for the iniquity of a child; the righteousness of the righteous shall be his own, and the wickedness of the wicked shall be his own" (Ezek 18:20).

The idea of resurrection might also have been partly the product of martyrdom. In the final stages of the Greek Empire, and the early days of the Roman Empire, the remnant of Jews that had returned from their exile in Babylon to rebuild the second temple under Ezra faced constant military threats, not only to their peace but to their very existence. Vastly outnumbered, they fought courageously against their would-be oppressors, and many of them died heroically. How could a God of justice permit their deaths? How could God abandon to oblivion those who were willing to give their lives for the honor of God's name?[2] With some basis in their scriptures, and some exposure to the ideas of immortality in other traditions, the Jews began to clarify how the *individual's* hope, and not simply the *nation's* hope, was in God: "But the souls of the righteous are in the hand of God, and no torment will ever touch them. In the eyes of the foolish they seem to have died, and their departure was thought to be a disaster, and their going from us to be their destruction; but they are at peace. For though in the sight of others they were punished, they will receive great good, because God tested them and found them worthy of himself" (Wis 3:1–5).

Distinguishing itself from Greek ideas of immortality, however, the Jewish understanding of resurrection was unabashedly corporeal. Rather than a doctrine of an immortal soul being released from its destructible body, Jewish thinking about resurrection included the *reconstitution of the complete person*, body and soul, at the end of time. While there were vague ideas about a spiritual existence between historical death and ultimate resurrection (see Jesus' story about the rich man and Lazarus in Luke 16:19–31), resurrection was a holistic idea that included the body. The bodily conditions would be somewhat altered, though, with the body being imbued with the same kind of immortality that the soul might be thought to have. Jesus is reported to have said, countering the Sadducee's doubt in the resurrection, that in the resurrection we "neither marry nor are given in marriage, but are like angels in heaven" (Mark 12:18–27), and Paul states that the dead "will be raised imperishable" (1 Cor 15:50–58).

The bodily nature of the resurrection in Jewish and early Christian theology is important in establishing what those authors whose works are included in the New Testament believed they were referring to when they talked about the resurrection of Jesus. Paul, whose writings predate

---

2. Crenshaw, "Love Is Stronger than Death," 71–72.

The Resurrection of History

the Gospels by several decades, talks about the "appearances" of the resurrected Jesus, but always in a fashion that differentiates these from either a ghostly presence (as in the case of the postmortem appearance of Samuel, conjured for Saul: see 1 Sam 28:7–20) or a revivification of someone recently deceased (as in the case of the widow's son: see Luke 7:11–17). Paul maintains "a firm and sharply delineated belief in a past event, the resurrection of Jesus of Nazareth."[3] The Gospels of course depict the resurrection of Jesus as an event in time, a couple of days after the crucifixion of Jesus. The resurrected Jesus spoke with his disciples (Matt 28:16–20), ate with his disciples (Luke 24:36–42), and even bore the wounds of his crucifixion (John 20:24–29). There would be some justification for saying that it wasn't the *nature* of Jesus' resurrection that was so shocking to the disciples—after all, if Jesus was a righteous person, God would raise him in vindication with all the martyrs and righteous dead—as the *timing* of it. Jesus' end-of-time resurrection, the early Christians said, happened during the course of time, in history, as if to mark out the beginning of the end time.

At least as far as the New Testament documents depict it, the announcement of the resurrection of Jesus was at the very heart of the early Christians' proclamation. The resurrection of Jesus is the climax of all four canonical Gospels (Matt 28:5; Mark 16:6; Luke 25:5; John 20:18), and Jesus' own predictions of the resurrection are a recurring motif within each Gospel (Matt 12:40; 16:21; 17:22; 19:17; 26:32; Mark 8:31; 9:31; 10:34; 14:28; Luke 9:22; 18:33; John 10:17; 14:19; 16:16). The apostolic proclamation identified in the Acts of the Apostles is the vindication of Jesus' ministry by means of God raising Jesus to new life (Acts 2:32–36; 10:34–43; 17:16–31). The dependence of the believers' new life "in Christ" on the resurrection and exaltation of Jesus is a central theme in most of Paul's letters (2 Cor 4:13–17; Eph 1:3–14; Phil 2:5–13; Col 3:1–4; 2 Tim 2:8–13). Even the Apocalypse repeatedly identifies "the Lamb who was slain" with "the Living One," the one "who was, and is, and is to come" (Rev 4:1–11). Throughout the New Testament, the death of Jesus is portrayed as an ordinarily shameful end to Jesus' life—except for the extraordinary raising of Jesus to new life. The resurrection of Jesus was taken to be God's seal of approval on Jesus' proclamation of God's reign, and God's own proclamation concerning human destiny (Rom 1:1–6; Acts 4:1–12; 1 Pet 1:3–9). Once again, the historical *claim* that Jesus was raised from the dead can be disputed by historians, but

---

3. Wright, *Resurrection of the Son of God*, 374.

we should from the outset recognize that the canonical Christian scriptures are unanimous in ascribing central theological significance to that claim.

While it can be argued that the Christian tradition has changed in many respects over its twenty centuries, the historical eventfulness of the resurrection of Jesus has been consistently affirmed, and this has been directly connected to the understanding of the resurrection as a bodily event. There is certainly little doubt that the Christian authors of the first and second centuries CE affirmed the bodily resurrection of Jesus against the Docetic view that the Son of God never actually took human form. It is clear that by the beginning of the second century, leading figures such as Ignatius declared belief in the bodily resurrection of Jesus as absolutely essential to Christian faith.[4] Later in the second century, it is still apparent that the church understood the term "resurrection" as bodily. Tertullian argued that since we are told by the apostles that Jesus experienced *resurrection*, it must have been bodily; therefore, he goes on to say, our future resurrection will be bodily as well, although our bodies will be animated not by natural principles but by "spiritual" principles, through the agency of the Holy Spirit.[5]

In the early third century, Origen defended the Gospel accounts of the empty tomb. Origen argued that Christianity is a faith founded on the acts of God in history, every bit as much as Judaism. For Origen, the New Testament reports of Jesus' bodily resurrection are historical accounts that can be examined and critiqued. Because they all report, in their various ways, the same event, Origen tends to regard them as comprising a single historical record, standing or falling together. Origen, while confident of the historical value of the Gospel accounts, struggles with questions regarding the nature of what they report, and feels compelled to qualify his claim to Jesus' bodily resurrection in order to maintain its historicity.[6]

In the fourth century, living in the newly powerful and newly privileged post-Constantine church, Athanasius engaged in a very different kind of historical reasoning. He assumed that since God was sovereign, there must be some sort of ultimate morality to the march of history. His understanding of what constituted historical evidence for the resurrection included the miracles wrought by the apostles in Jesus' name, the subsequent destruction of Jerusalem, the diminishing of pagan religions,

---

4. Ignatius, *Letter to the Smyrnaeans*, 3 (ANF 1:87).
5. Tertullian, *Five Books against Marcion*, 5.9 (ANF 3:447–49).
6. Origen, *Against Celsus*, 2.52 (ANF 1:456).

the fulfillment of prophecies from the Hebrew Scriptures, the past courage of martyrs, the chastity of virgins, the consistency of the resurrection with Greek metaphysical categories, and the widespread acceptance of Christian faith:

> For although the Greeks have told all manner of false tales, yet they were not able to feign a Resurrection of their idols—for it never crossed their mind, whether it be at all possible for the body again to exist after death.[7]

In the early fifth century, Augustine labored long over the concept of resurrection, dealing with questions such as the possibility of the reconstitution of the parts of a disintegrated human body for its future resurrection. His assumption seems to be that if intellectual objections to the bodily nature of resurrection can be met, people will happily embrace the historical resurrection of Jesus: "But if they do not believe that these miracles were wrought by Christ's apostles to gain credence to their preaching of His resurrection and ascension, this one grand miracle suffices for us, that the whole world has believed without any miracles."[8] Both Athanasius and Augustine inferred the *historical* dimension of the resurrection from its *historic* dimension, entering into evidence for the historical eventfulness of the resurrection the fact that something so initially incredible had come to be believed so widely. While this is certainly something that would be considered out-of-bounds by present-day historians, it is important for the present discussion to note that it is still the *historical* nature of the resurrection that is being talked about here.

By the thirteenth century, various conflicts including the Crusades had brought Christians into large-scale engagement with the Muslim world. This brought the historical claims for the Christian faith, and the resurrection in particular, into significant doubt for the first time in eight hundred years. These developments may have prompted some of the detailed reflections of Thomas Aquinas, who once again approached the question of the nature of the event that is testified to by the Gospels. Thomas asserts that Jesus rose in a state of glory with specific properties that were attributable from both theological considerations and analysis of the Gospel accounts of Jesus' resurrection. There is something new developing here: whereas in most previous analyses the bodily nature of the resurrection supports an

---

7. Athanasius, *Incarnation of the Word of God*, 50 (NPNF2 4:63–64).
8. Augustine, *City of God*, 22.5 (NPNF1 2:481–82).

argument for its historical nature, here the historical nature of the resurrection, firmly assumed, is used to support the argument as to its bodily nature. For Thomas, there is a full complementarity of the bodily dimension of the resurrection and the historicity of the resurrection, each helping to explain the other. Using great subtlety, Thomas says, "The individual arguments taken alone are not sufficient proof of Christ's resurrection but taken together, in a cumulative way, they *manifest it* perfectly."[9] The Protestant Reformers, for all their distaste for the scholastics, share with Thomas a high regard for Augustine's certainty as to the bodily resurrection of Jesus. Calvin says, "But it is to be observed, in passing, that when he is said to have 'risen from the dead,' these terms express the reality both of his death and resurrection, as if it had been said, that he died the same death as other men naturally die, and received immortality in the same mortal flesh which he had assumed."[10]

It is unquestionable that the majority of Christians through the centuries have believed that the resurrection of Jesus involved the transformation of his body, and it is almost as safe to say that the majority of New Testament scholars today, whatever their *personal* beliefs, will agree that the New Testament depicts some kind of bodily resurrection of Jesus. Thomas F. Torrance sums up the larger historical Christian tradition on the proclamation of the bodily nature of the resurrection when he says, "Everything depends on the resurrection of the body, otherwise all we have is a Ghost for a Saviour."[11]

CAN A CHRISTIAN DOUBT THE RESURRECTION?

There is an old philosophical riddle that goes like this. A wooden ship sails the seas for several years, and one of its boards needs replacing. The board is replaced and the ship sails on. A while later, another board is replaced for reasons of wear and tear, and then another, and another, until, after many years, every board on the ship has been replaced. The riddle is, when is the ship a new ship? When the first board is replaced? When half the boards have been replaced? When the last board has been replaced? Never?

---

9. Aquinas, *Summa Theologiae*, III, Q55, Art. 6. Italics throughout are original to the quoted material.

10. Calvin, *Institutes*, 2.16.13.

11. Torrance, *Space, Time, and Resurrection*, 87.

The Resurrection of History

There are certain elements of Christian belief and practice that have been altered over the years. At some point, in the Western Church at least, the rule that married men could serve as priests was replaced with a rule that only celibate men could serve as priests (something which the Reformation sought to reverse). At some point, the belief that the earth was the physical center of the universe gave way to a heliocentric model in which the earth revolved around the sun. More recently, the belief that the Mass could not be celebrated in the vernacular and still be valid was overturned, causing widespread change in liturgical practice. All of these elements of the Christian faith were considered nonessential; even with these changes, the ship remained the ship.

Paul is adamant that the ship of Christian teaching must include the historicity of the resurrection (though we will encounter important arguments about its precise nature in chapters to follow). To the Christians in Corinth, Paul writes:

> Now if Christ is proclaimed as raised from the dead, how can some of you say there is no resurrection of the dead? If there is no resurrection of the dead, then Christ has not been raised; and if Christ has not been raised, then our proclamation has been in vain and your faith has been in vain. We are even found to be misrepresenting God, because we testified that he raised Christ—whom he did not raise if it is true that the dead are not raised. For if the dead are not raised, then, Christ has not been raised. If Christ has not been raised, your faith is futile and you are still in your sins. Then those also who have died in Christ have perished. If for this life only we have hope in Christ, we are of all people most to be pitied. (1 Cor 15:12–18)

The author of the letter to the Hebrews refers to "the God of peace, who brought back from the dead our Lord Jesus, the great shepherd of the sheep, by the blood of the eternal covenant" (Heb 13:20); Peter says of Jesus that "through him you have come to trust in God, who raised him from the dead and gave him glory" (1 Pet 1:21); all New Testament writers refer to Jesus as being alive, and about to come again in glory. The hope of the Christian, according to these authors, seems to be predicated on the resurrection of Jesus. Can something that appears so key to the Christian message and so universally shared in the apostolic age be negotiable in ours?

In the last few centuries, the Renaissance, the discovery of the New World, the Reformation, the Enlightenment, the rise of the scientific paradigm, the industrial revolution, the harnessing of electricity, the rise of socialism, the adoption of the evolutionary paradigm, the invention of modern aeronautics, two pan-European armed conflicts, the unleashing of nuclear power, the technological revolution, and now the dawn of the information age have all served to underscore change as the only constant in the mind of the contemporary Westerner. Is it possible that doctrines once thought indispensable to Christian faith could be replaced with new ones, and that the claim that the resurrection of Jesus is a historical event can be dispensed with as a relic of a bygone era? There are many theologians who say that this can be done, should be done, and must be done, if Christian faith is to have any credibility in its third millennium. In this view, the greatest service that contemporary theologians can do for their forebears is to do as they have done, and adapt the basic symbols of the Christian faith to current conceptualities.

On the other hand, there are others who argue that the durability of Christian doctrine in the context of massive intellectual and social upheaval is one of the church's greatest gifts to the twenty-first century. The continuity of what the church proclaims—even if practices alter—not only provides some sense of stability in uncertain times, but it also serves as offering continuity with what was understood and taught by Jesus himself. The early church, as contemporaries and eyewitnesses of Jesus, would have endeavored to proclaim Jesus on his own terms, and remain faithful to his understanding of God and God's workings in the world, and so should we. In this view, it is up to the church to engage scholarship of every kind and discover ways to faithfully maintain its teaching as the teaching of Jesus, being careful to find points of agreement with and distinction from contemporary ideas in every new era.

This debate isn't new to the twenty-first century, but with the waning of the authority of Christianity as the dominant cultural force in Western culture, the historical claims of the early church have been held up for examination in a way not seen since the first centuries of the church's existence. What has gone unnoticed by many, however, is that the debate over how to deal with the resurrection of Jesus has been affected by the ground shifting under historians' feet. What is considered to be sound historical method has undergone its own dialectical evolution, and this has affected—sometimes consciously, other times unconsciously—how theologians deal with the historical dimension of the resurrection of Jesus. What has happened over the last few decades, I believe, is the revival of a fuller, more robust understanding of historical method and the process of historical reconstruction, offering a renewed opportunity for contemporary theologians to assist the church in proclaiming the historical resurrection of Jesus.

There will be many who read what follows and will still not be prepared to assert that the resurrection of Jesus needs to be proclaimed as a historical event. It is likely that this very issue must have been at play among Christians at the end of the first century, when the story of Thomas's doubt was recirculated in the Gospel of John. While the Gospel writer's point of view on the resurrection of Jesus is clear, the story is related with a great deal of sympathy to those who find it hard to believe. Thomas is not portrayed as stupid, stubborn, or sinful: he is the one who, earlier in this same Gospel, is willing to meet his end with Jesus in Jerusalem, if that's what loyalty demands. Thomas is not disowned by the other disciples, and is not shunned by Jesus. Jesus comes and makes a point of approaching Thomas, and it is Thomas who in the end offers one of the most profound expressions of faith in the entire New Testament: having come to believe that Jesus was in fact resurrected from the dead, he proclaims, "My Lord and my God!"

What follows is dedicated to all the Thomases among us, and the Thomas in every one of us, because with Thomas we know right down to our bones that history matters.

QUESTIONS FOR CONSIDERATION

Seminary

1. How would you describe the evolution from the notion of *collective* immortality to the notion of *individual* mortality?
2. How does the idea of resurrection reflect the image of God as being just?

Study Group

1. What scriptural stories, ideas, or quotes come to mind when you consider how history matters to our understanding of God?
2. What difference do you think belief in Jesus' resurrection made to the apostles and the early church?

Individual

1. What would you offer to someone in your parish or congregation who said they didn't believe in life after death?
2. When does believing in the resurrection seem easy? When does it seem hard?

3 The History of History

WE ALL HAVE OUR likes and dislikes when it comes to what comes out of Hollywood, and sometimes those likes and dislikes emerge as responses to the very same production.

When *Braveheart* came out, I was delighted that the historic conflict between the Scottish and the English in the early fourteenth century was going to be highlighted. I was sure that some elements of it would be over-romanticized (and I was right), but people seldom line up around the block to see a purely historical documentary. In case you missed it, *Braveheart* traced the paramilitary career of William Wallace, whose personal skill in the battlefield was matched perhaps only by his ability to rouse the common folk to stand up to their better-heeled and better-armed oppressors.

There were certain elements that any good Scottish tour guide will point out to have been unhistorical—that is, without any basis in what is normally considered to be historical evidence. For instance, in the film William Wallace is depicted as having had a romantic fling with the English princess Isabella, even though Isabella was a child and living in France at the time. In order to depict Wallace as more thoroughly heroic by Anglo-American audiences, there was no depiction of Wallace forcing peasants into armed service through conscription, although this is a well-attested historical fact. To bring together past events and present images of Scottish culture, the Wallace of *Braveheart* and his contemporaries were wearing tartan kilts and painted their faces blue and white, although these are both anachronisms. In the largest battle scene, as at his death, Wallace lifts up freedom as the goal of this epic struggle when, truth be told, it is likely that most Scots at the time wouldn't have cared who ruled them, so long as they were left in peace to tend their flocks and taxes weren't too high! Finally, cutting me to the heart, was the depiction of Robert the Bruce as weak-willed and treacherous, when most biographers of my great ancestor depict him as a strategic thinker, a friend of Wallace, and the victim of betrayal (by his own father).

So where is the harm, it can be asked, if a Hollywood film takes liberty with historical research? In fact, isn't it a *good* thing if Wallace the commoner is elevated above Bruce the landed aristocrat? And what is history actually *for*, anyway? Is it so disinterested scholars can lay out a lifeless litany of names, places, and dates for generations of hapless high-schoolers to memorize, or is it to bring ancient heroes to life to inspire us by their virtues and exploits? Are we more interested in discovering what people of other times and places felt, thought, taught, and experienced, or in raising up unassailable models of current values for or present purposes? If we agree that history matters, we will want to ask both *how* it matters and *for what* it matters. Specifically, we will want to ask questions of this kind about the New Testament accounts of the resurrection of Jesus, to put into perspective any claims to their offering "historical" accounts.

ANCIENT HISTORY WRITING

History, it is said, is written by the winners. While not always true, it is certainly the case that most history writing in ancient times was done in or close to sources of power and wealth. *Traditional* history writing was a function of the royal or imperial court, where relevant records were kept and educated people could be employed as librarians, copyists, and legal experts. Traditional history writing sought to connect the present cultural structures and practices with some sacred past, often shrouded in myth and mystery. According to Ernst Breisach, perhaps the world's foremost expert on the art of history writing, ancient Indian histories show little interest in precisely dating events, or in distinguishing fantasy and fact, let alone identifying elements of any historical method as it wove the divine and the mundane. Ancient Chinese history writing, on the other hand, was entirely concrete and particular, but was always preoccupied with linking the rise and fall of dynasties and rulers to their observance to a timeless moral code."[1]

In Western cultures, for the most part ancient historians were just as concerned with legitimizing the current reign of whomever was in power by means of genealogy, tales of battles won, and/or the imposition of some

---

1. Breisach, "Historiography: an Overview," 4025–26.

divine seal of approval. Biography, a key genre of history writing, focused on individuals with the intention of holding them up to scrutiny based on their moral successes and failures. While it was widely understood that most if not all history writing was somehow supported by some wealthy patron (as live theatre productions are today), it was still considered legitimizing to any historical account for the writer to at least state who *wasn't* funding the telling of the tale at hand. Although traditional historians of ancient times may have typically been more trusting of their sources than present-day historians are, they were keen to present themselves as free from biases that might bring their work into disrepute.[2]

In some important respects, history writing in ancient Greece represented an important development of what had come before it. The fifth-century BCE historian Thucydides, for instance, turned his attention away from the then-current art of refining written mythologies to the practice of establishing reliable accounts of relatively recent events, ones that could be attested to by eyewitnesses. As historiographer Arnoldo Momigliano put it, "The choice between what is true and what is untrue, or at least between what is probable and what is improbable, was inherent in the profession of the historian as the Greeks understood it."[3] This concern for historical verification in Greek history writing was passed onto the Romans, upheld by no less than the great statesman Cicero in the first century BCE: "Who does not know history's first law to be that an author must not dare tell anything but the truth? And the second law that he must make bold to tell the whole truth?"[4]

The writings that form the majority of the New Testament, including the Gospels and most of the Epistles, are clearly influenced by these concerns. Even though they refer to and even narrate events that sound unusual to our third-millennium sensibilities, such as miracles, exorcisms, and the resurrection of the dead, they constantly invoke eyewitness testimony, including that of those living at the time of the writing (cf. 1 Cor 15:1–8; 1 Pet 1:8 and 5:1; Luke 1:1–4; John 21:24; 1 John 1:1). According to R. A. Burridge, who conducted a quantitative analysis of surviving Graeco-Roman biographies, the Gospels fall comfortably within the genre of ancient biography, which commonly included such literary elements as

---

2. Clark, *History, Theory, Text*, 166.
3. Momigliano, *Classical Foundations*, 19.
4. Breisach, *Historiography*, 57.

ancestry, birth narratives, stories of boyhood and education, great deeds, evidences of virtue, death, and postmortem impact.[5]

An anthropological lens, applied to the Gospels, would suggest that they are the outcroppings of a reasonably unified, self-correcting *oral* tradition that allows for variations in emphasis while still concerned for fidelity to originating sources.[6] This wasn't simply on the order of community gossip, but rather, in keeping with the practice of religious communities of that time, this would be the province of skilled and probably *trained* persons upon whom the early Christian community would rely on to accurately remember and hand on the stories and saying of Jesus:

> It seems to be an extremely tenaciously-held misapprehension among exegetes that any early Christian author must *either* be a purposeful theologian and writer *or* a fairly reliable historian. . . . This is a false alternative. . . . The fact of the early Christian Apostles, teachers, and Evangelists having presented their material with a religious end in view does not necessarily mean *per se* that their memories ceased to function, or that their respect for historical facts vanished.[7]

In the first few centuries of the church's existence, authors such as Ignatius, Irenaeus, and Origen argued against skeptics for the historicity of the Gospel accounts on grounds of evidence rather than divine authority. Whatever else they may have believed about the divine inspiration of the authors of the Gospels, they felt compelled to counter their opponents to present arguments based on consistency, coherency, and the motivations of those reputed to be eyewitnesses. The church "fathers" certainly regarded the Gospels (and particular claims found in the Epistles) as public historical documentation. As most of us know, however, today it is often said that the Gospels are theological documents rather than historical documents. What does that mean, and how did this understanding of the Gospels evolve?

MEDIEVAL AND EARLY MODERN HISTORIOGRAPHY

As the Roman Empire began to crumble in the first few centuries CE, the Christian church became the central source of that history writing which

---

5. Burridge, *What Are the Gospels?*, 258.
6. Vansina, *Oral Tradition as History*, 159.
7. Gerhardsson, *Memory and Manuscript*, 71.

endured into later centuries. With the diminishing need to defend its historical accounts, the church developed a historical method which, while recalling the need for facticity and the importance of eyewitness accounts, adopted a practical deference to certain authorities, including the writings of the Jewish scriptures and what would become the official Christian scriptures. Respect for Augustine's dynamic, open-ended view of history effectively overruled attempts to theologically establish cyclical views of history. The lack of any significant challenge to this view may have had the long-term effect of reducing history writing to the chronicling of civil and ecclesiastical authorities on the one hand, and the production of relatively uncritical hagiographies (lives of saints) on the other. The flow of history was not regarded so much as a river running its purposeful course to its natural destination as the ebb and flow of the ocean, with occasional storms of divine activity. In such a setting it is not surprising to find that it was believed that

> God's will, not human will, governed human events, and hence every event was the result of divine planning and not simply the effects of preceding conditions or human actions. The modern concept of history as a chain of causes and effects, where a given state of affairs results necessarily from its antecedents, was in general foreign to medieval historiography.[8]

As the feudal system of the Middle Ages began to break down in the eleventh and twelfth centuries, the increased use of migrant labor increased the use of money and credit in Italy and central Europe. This "new" means of storing wealth led in turn to the capitalization of property and hunting, fishing, and logging rights that had previously been held in families for hundreds of years.[9] The increasing selling and purchasing of land in turn produced the need to properly document transactions, including deeds of ownership, which in turn led to a revival of interest in archaeology (inscriptions on cornerstones and the like) and textual provenance (where a deed came from, who signed it, who kept it, etc.). Gradually, the long-neglected practices of gathering historical *evidence* worked their way back into common parlance. In the sixteenth century, Luther was able to challenge the reigning method of appealing to the divine authority of the church for verification of competing religious claims with a more humanistic call to compare current ecclesiastical practices against the "deed" of the church,

---

8. Breisach, *Historiography*, 127–28.
9. House, *Francis*, 29.

The History of History

the New Testament documents, interpreted without the bias of present ecclesiastical patronage.

The implications of this move were almost certainly larger than were recognized at the time. Challenging the church effectively uncoupled the *what is* of historical events from *what God wills*. In science, there was the parallel rise of "inductive method" described by the seventeenth-century scholar Francis Bacon that sought to reason from "bare facts" in themselves rather than rely on previously named categories.[10] By the end of the seventeenth century, Europe embraced Peter Bayle's *Historical and Critical Dictionary* in which historical truth was said to be not a function of the historian's intellect but something inherent in historical facts themselves.[11] In this new intellectual climate, which featured weakened papal authority, completing claims to God's favor in times of war among European nations became a theological dilemma: how was God's favor to be written into *any* historical account with certainty?[12] In the eighteenth century, by the critical minds of Voltaire and *les philosophes* in France and David Hume in England, all claims to divine favor and authority came under the lens of historical criticism, including those in holy scripture. Identification of the "laws" of reason and of nature in the works of Descartes, Newton, and others fostered a climate in which interpretive frameworks such as Comte's vision of humanity's movement from theological through metaphysical to modern categories or Hegel's dialectical idealism could flourish, and history came to be viewed not so much the arena of God's freedom as the arena of natural necessity. Breisach dryly notes that after a century or two of celebrating the relative independence of historical "facts," new interpretive schema descended as various attempts to define the "laws" of history were made, and the study of history was overtaken by a relatively rote process of handing down from one generation to another the historical system of some great historian. By the end of the eighteenth century, history writing had been *re-traditionalized*.[13]

10. Bacon, *Novum Organum Scientiarum* (originally published 1620).
11. Bayle, *Historical and Critical Dictionary: Selections* (originally published 1695).
12. See the discussion in Tilley, *History, Theology, and Faith*, 71–73.
13. Breisach, *Historiography*, 199.

MODERN HISTORIOGRAPHY

In the nineteenth century, Leopold von Ranke, often hailed as the "father of modern history," instituted what became known as "the seminar method." Harkening back to the sixteenth and seventeenth centuries, he encouraged his students to move beyond ready-made, synthesized accounts and seek out any and all relevant documentation and physical evidence, and engage in free-ranging debate over the significance of these "primary" sources in an emulation of inductive scientific method. Von Ranke is perhaps best known for declaring that the goal of historical inquiry is to understand the past "how it actually was," that is, to enter into the perspective of a past era, suspending moral judgment long enough to appreciate the past on its own terms.

Johann Gustav Droysen and Max Weber also emphasized the intellectual freedom of the historian, and the historian's duty to allow the evidence to shape the historian's perspective (rather than the other way around). Droysen helpfully outlined key dimensions of the historian's subsequent interpretive task, giving a fuller description of the data that historians actually consider. (1) The *pragmatic* interpretation concentrated on the immediate aims of the principal actors in the historical episode at hand. (2) The *conditional* interpretation stressed the material conditions within which the episode unfolded. (3) The *psychological* interpretation focused on the character and personality of those involved. (4) The *ethical* interpretation considered the material, ideal, and practical spheres of the moral life in relation to the events under study.[14] Weber believed that the construction of "ideal types" could be a useful technique for the historian, even if no historical example perfectly met the requirements of the paradigm. Weber also stressed, however, that such ideal types were useful if and only if the historian remembered that these types were the historian's own constructions, and not verifiable facts in and of themselves.[15] Perhaps of greatest importance to both Droysen and Weber was the methodological separation of the historian from the historical evidence requiring interpretation.

Twentieth-century historians, following on the efforts of nineteenth-century scholars, held a variety of opinions on the role of the historian in history writing. R. G. Collingwood identified the goal of the historian as discovering human intention. He understood that the "historian himself

---

14. Droysen, *Grundriss der Historik*, 19–24
15. Shils and Finch, *Max Weber on the Meaning of the Social Sciences*, 43–46.

is part of the process he is studying," but rather than believing that the historian's involvement would *obscure* the data, he believed it would serve to *illuminate* the data, because of the congruence between the historian's mind and the mind of the historical figure(s) being investigated, that is, the subject and the object of historical inquiry.[16] Marcel Bloch, a French historian arrested for his involvement in resistance to the Nazis, went even further, asserting that historical facts, unlike scientific facts, are in essence *psychological* facts, that is, they exist in the mind of the historian.[17] In an era where scientific determinism was a much-debated subject, Bloch was insistent on underlining that human freedom is the ever-present variable in human history: the conditions for good or for evil are to be distinguished from the causes of human action—including those of the historian. Edward Hallett Carr agreed with Collingwood and Bloch on the need to factor the historian into the process of history writing, and spoke of history writing as "a continuous process of interaction between the historian and his facts, an unending dialogue between the present and the past."[18] Writing after the popularization of Marxist theory, psychoanalysis, and operant conditioning, Carr extended Collingwood's vision of the object of history writing to include the *unconscious* as well as the conscious intentions of historical figures, hoping that historians could contribute to the discernment of the larger cause-and-effect structures within historical reality.[19] The extreme version of this search to uncover the perennial principles of historical process came to be labeled "historicism."

As the mid-twentieth-century Cold War developed, however, there was a notable reaction in the West against anything that seemed consistent with the historical determinism of Marxist theory referenced by the Soviet Union. Karl Popper argued that since the course of human history is affected by the growth in human knowledge, and since growth in human knowledge is in principle presently unknowable, we cannot therefore predict the future course of human history. Popper completed the circuit, so to speak, by saying, "I wish to defend the view, so often attacked by historicists, that *history is characterized by its interest in actual, singular, or specific events, rather than in laws or generalizations.*"[20] G. R. Elton spoke along the

16. Collingwood, *Idea of History*, 248.
17. Bloch, *Historian's Craft*, 194.
18. Carr, *What Is History?*, 35.
19. Ibid., 111.
20. Popper, *Poverty of Historicism*, 3–5.

same lines when he said, "History is 'idiographic,' that is, it particularizes, and not 'nomothetic,' that is, designed to establish general laws."[21] Elton repudiated the characterization of the historian's enterprise as the creation of grand interpretive schemes. Connecting medieval history writing to twentieth-century history writing, he remarked, "When Mr. Carr, and others, seek a purpose in history, they are trying to fill a vacuum created when God was removed from history."[22]

POSTMODERN HISTORY WRITING

For a variety of reasons—the Vietnam War, Watergate, growing interest in apartheid, increased tensions in the Middle East, etc., etc.—interest among Western historians in the late twentieth century turned from the search for grand interpretive schemes to implications of the admission that historians are never free from their own conscious or unconscious individual interpretive frameworks. This concern in the discipline of history writing was part of a larger philosophical approach to literature, the arts, and the social sciences known as "postmodernism." If modernism, from von Ranke through to Elton, can be characterized as the search for the proper *object* of history writing, that is, the elusive historical "fact" or "scheme," postmodernism can be characterized as the search for the proper *subject* of history, that is, the elusive creature known as "the historian."

Hayden White suggested that the common thread of all history writing, from Greek drama through medieval hagiography to demonstrations of dialectical materialism, is the drive to share human meaning in *narrative* form: "The demand for closure in the historical story is a demand, I suggest, for moral meaning, a demand that sequences of real events be assessed as to their significance as elements of a moral drama."[23] Since human beings live in time, and understand themselves in narrative terms, historical writing creates historical events from past events by structuring them in narrative form. Once historical events are created, they become regarded as "actual" events that are incorporated into further narrative constructions. Echoing Collingwood, White does not see this tendency as illegitimate: since history is about human actions, and human beings live narratively, it is natural that the meaning of human actions is understood narratively. If White is

21. Elton, *Practice of History*, 26.
22. Ibid., 40.
23. White, *Content of the Form*, 21.

correct, though, we might well pause to ask, What is history? Is it poetry? Is it literature? Is it myth-making? Is it simply the projection of the historian's perspective anachronistically onto past events and persons? Does such an assessment lead us to conclude that all history writing is ultimately idiosyncratic—there being as many histories as there are historians—and irredeemably unscientific, having nothing to do with actual historical events, except as hooks to hang our own individualized quests for meaning?

Postmodernism sees any claim to universality in historical writing as two-faced or duplicitous.[24] The vast mingling of the world's ethnicities in the past few decades has given rise to the awareness that there is no single, neutral, "reasonable" perspective that can be safely assumed by the world's peoples, even the world's scholars. In the twentieth century, the ascendancy of the United States as a global power challenged the older "first world" view of European supremacy, while in America the impact of the civil rights movement and the feminist movement challenged assumptions of white male superiority. As present-day Western historians seek to include African nations within a discipline rooted in Eurocentric assumptions as to what constitutes a society, a nation, or a civilization, it may be that assumptions around the role of money, marriage, or servitude effectively prevent historians from translating African experience into European terms.[25] The postmodern critique of any simple, empirical objectivity in history writing has served to name the ever-present danger of tacit prejudicial influences that unthinkingly privilege certain accepted narratives over others, something which can retard or even preclude new discoveries by effectively disallowing certain questions as unacceptable. While no doubt some may find this constricting, some find it liberating, as Elizabeth Clark does in her studies of the early church fathers:

> Among the "mental tools" that [postmodern] theory offers scholars of patristic Christianity are (1) an examination of "authorial function" that calls into question attributions of intention and context; (2) symptomatic and Derridean readings that attend to the gaps, absences, and *aporias* in texts; (3) ideology critique, especially helpful in unpacking the early Christian writers' representations of "Others," including women; and (4) postcolonial

---

24. Foucault, "What Is an Author?" I borrow the term "duplicitous" from Donald Bouchard's translation. The sinister connotations of the term "duplicitous" in the sense of involving deception as well as opacity, in my opinion, provide the undertone of Foucault's disdain for uncritical confidence in the use of contemporary historical method.

25. Feierman, "Africa in History, 45.

discourse theory that helps to illuminate the ways in which Christianity and Empire intertwined.[26]

In other words, deliberately *un-knowing* what "everybody knows" by asking "What do other people know?" can free the historian into reexamining existing texts and making new discoveries.

Postmodernism also sees any claim to final comprehension of a text to be duplicitous. Since most history writing depends in whole or in part on previously written texts, in the simple case of someone reading a historian's work it is true that (1) no observer completely recalls what they saw; (2) no author completely records everything they recall; (3) no historian completely comprehends what they find recorded; (4) no historian completely reports everything they comprehend; and (5) no reader of the historians work completely comprehends what the historian reports. Roland Barthes shone a light on our tendency to believe that the object of reading any text—history writing included—is to understand the author. The author of any text cannot, however, truly be discovered through the text, because "the text is a tissue of quotations drawn from the innumerable centres of culture."[27] That is, there are so many influences on a text, so many assumptions embedded in a text, so many allusions springing from a text, that no one can say once and for all what any text really and finally *means*, so it must be admitted that it is *the reader that supplies meaning to the text*: "The birth of the reader must be at the cost of the death of the Author."[28] It no doubts serves well for any historian to remember that all history writing has its limitations, and that no text is ever *fully* and *finally* understood. If importing interpretive theories is inevitable, says historian Richard Evans, fuller awareness of these theories and the multiplicity of potential interpretive theories can and should be part of any thorough history writing: "The real question at issue here is *what enables us* to read a source 'against the grain,' and here theory does indeed come in."[29]

And postmodernism sees any claim to absolute freedom of interpretation as duplicitous. All history writing presumes, in its selection and presentation of material, some parameters of relevance—but who sets these parameters? Every act of history writing presumes some conscious

---

26. Clark, *History, Theory, Text*, 170.
27. Barthes, *Image, Music, Text*, 146.
28. Ibid., 148.
29. Evans, *In Defense of History*, 83. Here Evans references Derrida's *Of Grammatology, Writing and Difference, Positions,* and *Dissemination*.

The History of History

or unconscious metanarrative within which history writing makes sense. For George Santayana, the metanarrative in which history should be written is that of universal Progress: "Progress, far from consisting in change, depends on retentiveness. . . . When experience is not retained, as among savages, infancy is perpetual. Those who cannot remember the past are condemned to repeat it."[30] Someone whose worldview is governed by the metanarrative of the unstoppable progress of humanism might include the promulgation of the United Nations' Universal Declaration of Human Rights as central event in his or her history of the twentieth century, but someone whose worldview is governed by the metanarrative of the inevitability of the environmental degradation of the planet might not. Relevance is determined by the "discourse"—the larger academic or cultural conversation—in which any particular history writing effort finds itself involved, and each discourse is governed by one metanarrative or another. But due to the breakdown of cultural and ethnic isolation brought about by increased movements of human populations, there does not appear to be one clear metanarrative governing all discourses. Some historians, like Carr, citing the loss of such certainty in times past, call for historians to join in the bold search for a new, universally acceptable metanarrative, rather than pretend we can do without one:

> This was the age of innocence, and historians walked in the Garden of Eden, without a scrap of philosophy to cover them, naked and unashamed before the god of history. Since then, we have known Sin and experienced a Fall; and those historians who today pretend to dispense with a philosophy of history are merely trying, vainly and self-consciously, like members of a nudist colony, to recreate the Garden of Eden in their garden suburb.[31]

Michel Foucault, on the other hand, decried the tendency of elitist peer-pressure to determine the acceptable parameters of discourse, especially if it resulted in the homogenization of the thought of great and prolific thinkers, creating a "canonical" standard of interpretation.[32]

It is true that any discourse is to some extent—perhaps even a large extent—self-referencing and self-sustaining. Self-justification is an observable human tendency, whether at the level of the individual, the corporation, or the larger cultural context. This tendency by itself, however,

---

30. Santayana, *Life of Reason*, 284.
31. Carr, *What Is History?*, 21.
32. Foucault, "What Is an Author?," 124

45

The Resurrection of History

does not disable any given discourse from actually relating to that which is external to itself. Just because a given discourse promotes a particular view of historical reality doesn't mean that it isn't in touch with historical reality. While the challenge of postmodernism to the naïve confidence of historians has been effective and to some extent chastening, few present-day historians have quit the pursuit of historical truth. Joyce Appleby, Lynn Hunt, and Margaret Jacob represent, I think, the majority of Western historians in the early twenty-first century when they "accept the objectivity of objects and consider the objects' frequent resistance to accurate representations as an invitation to further investigation."[33] Even without a universally agreed-upon metanarrative or historical framework, the work of history writing goes on:

> Modern Westerners cannot live without causal language and generalizations about human behavior because these organize their reality. Without heuristic concepts of such things as nation, culture, class, ethnicity, education, global economy, the complexity of life would break down into a welter of isolated facts. People want to make sense of their world, even if explanations are proved to be necessarily partial.[34]

If the myth of a universal perspective on history has been obliterated by the postmodern critique, what is left? Can there be any agreement as to what is or is not historical? Are we faced with the "death" of history?

THIRD-MILLENNIUM HISTORY WRITING

I would suggest that the present state of history writing is more than a mere saw-off among various concerns. There is, in the West at least, an emerging practice of history writing that hasn't been fully articulated among professional historians but is starting to come into view. This practice promises to combine the strengths of previous approaches to history writing, and is one that I think lends itself to problematic texts such as those in the New Testament. Traditional history writing consciously embraced its metaphysical assumptions and its metanarrative. Modern history writing embraced the openness of modern science to allow facts and phenomena to challenge existing categories and frameworks. Postmodern history writing embraced

---

33. Appleby et al., *Telling the Truth about History*, 284–85.
34. Ibid., 305.

the inevitability of history writing employing less-than-universal assumptions and frameworks while demanding that these be made explicit for purposes of critique. What I will call "third millennium history writing" seeks to make its way cognizant of the developments within the discipline of history writing.

C. T. McIntire calls for a multi-dimensional approach to history writing, one that takes all of the above into account by encouraging historians to employ a historical method that references the historical dimension of any event with what he calls the structural and ultimate dimensions:

> Most broadly cast, my proposal is that reality—our world—exists according to three dimensions. . . . The *historical* dimension is the phenomenon identifiable as the temporal process coming into being, carrying on, modifying, perhaps developing, and then passing away. . . . The *structural* (or ontic) dimension of a phenomenon is the phenomenon identifiable as a structure or system with particular inner constitution of make-up. . . . The *ultimate* dimension is the phenomenon identifiable as a manifestation of the meaning of reality and as a disclosure of good and evil, alienation and liberation, sin and salvation.[35]

McIntire might be accused of expanding the historian's role into that of a philosopher or even a theologian, but I would argue that he is simply taking into account the legitimate criticisms of history writing that we have noted above. A historian has to consider the historical event not in isolation but in the cause-and-effect flow of sufficient conditions and freely undertaken actions, including their consequences. A historian has to consider what an historical event actually is, that is, that is, what *kind* of event something is, how that event takes place within structures, and what its constituent parts are. And a historian has to consider what interpretations the event is being subjected to in the very act of history writing, identifying its relationship to a given discourse, the assumptions built into the text reporting the event, and the metanarrative supplied by the historian. These requirements, McIntire claims, are just as applicable to the economist, the political scientist, the sociologist, the anthropologist, and the theologian as to the historian. And I would agree.

McIntire also stresses the fluid nature of historical events, saying that "contrary to popular wisdom, historical study is *not* simply about the past

---

35. McIntire, "Historical Study," 18–19.

but about past-present-future."[36] All historical events have a "pastness" to them, which gives them objectivity and allows them to be considered by more than one historian; they still need to be considered, as von Ranke would have counseled, in their place and time and historical authenticity. But all historical events also have a present character, as they are re-called from the past into the present, at least partially, for examination and appreciation; they need to be considered in their historic impact upon the present, which includes the impact made on the history writer. And all historical events have a futurity about them, as part of a process that leads through today into tomorrow; they need to be considered in their *value* as contributing to the betterment or degradation of the world according to the metanarrative employed by the historian considering the event. Today, offering any less would be disingenuous on the part of the self-aware historian.

If McIntire's approach is right-headed, it may be that a historian might consider his or her clear and certain religious orientation to be an advantage rather than a hindrance in history writing. Eric Cochrane, writing from his own perspective, says that a Catholic historian would have the advantages of (1) being sensitive to the role of religion and theology, which are nearly omnipresent in human affairs, (2) being open to the potency of human will to freely act no matter how constrained by circumstances, and (3) being faithful to the historian's *vocation* as a historian, to remain faithful to the discipline as an act of devotion to God. Finally, the Catholic historian would be honor-bound to retain a sense of humility about history writing as he or she, "while insisting upon the autonomy of history as a discipline, . . . will remember that history is not identical with the whole of reality."[37] No doubt other Christians, as well as Jews, Muslims, and believers of other faiths, could make similar and overlapping claims: religious belief does not disqualify anyone from history writing, but may in fact *empower* history writing.

This faith-friendly approach to history ironically makes up for what the postmodern critique found lacking in modern historical method: the identification of the sacred as an orientation to history writing. While much of traditional history writing in the ancient world consisted wholly in the orientation of the present to the past, Jewish history writing, affected by the experience of the Exile, developed a future-oriented eschatological

---

36. Ibid., 27.

37. Cochrane, "What Is Catholic Historiography?," 453–54.

dimension as well, by placing current events within, rather than at the end of, their metanarrative. As the World Council of Churches' document "God in Nature and History" put it:

> History for Israel was no longer part of nature. Unlike nature, it is directed towards a goal. . . . So Israel believed in the ultimate significance of her historical encounter with God; she believed that in this encounter the final reality was disclosed, and that this reality is the key to understanding of all things, in nature and history, from creation to consummation.[38]

Christians incorporated that view in most of their history writing, evaluating historical events in terms of their relative conformity to an ideal past (Eden) or an ideal future (Heaven). Maintaining that view required the foundational belief that the entire historical process is somehow governed by God. The disenchantment of nature that took place with the rise of modern science in the sixteenth and seventeenth centuries, combined with widespread rejection of the church's authority and questions about God's sovereignty, prompted Western scholarship to search for a new, or at least revised, metanarrative. A revival of cyclical views such as those of Giambattista Vico competed with progressivist views such as those of Hegel, but these failed to produce a widely accepted sense of meaning to contingent, historical existence. Dialectical materialism of the nineteenth and early twentieth century, taken within an evolutionary framework, denied *ultimate* significance to historical human struggle, and had no resources with which to remythologize human existence. Charles Taylor laments that the Christian metanarrative has been effectively displaced by a secular narrative that attempts to ascribe some sort of victory to modern science for having triumphed over religion:

> The narrative dimension is extremely important, because the force of these CWS [closed world systems] comes less from the supposed detailed argument (that science refutes religion, or that Christianity is incompatible with human rights), and much more from the general form of the narratives, to the effect that there was once a time when religion could flourish, but that time is past. . . . In a certain sense, the original arguments on which this narrative rests cease to matter, so powerful is the sense . . . that these old views just *can't* be options for us.[39]

---

38. World Council of Churches, "God in Nature and History," 296.
39. Taylor, *Secular Age*, 590.

The Resurrection of History

Udo Schnelle, in his *Theology of the New Testament*, brings together many of the elements of history writing involved in this "Third Milennimum" approach. He begins with the observation that we know that events are not *in themselves* history, because to become history they need historians doing history writing. Yet we don't give up on reference to actual events, because what we want insight into is the larger, actual reality we find ourselves to be a part of.

> Far and away more than law, philosophy, or political ideologies, religion claims to represent the one, all-encompassing reality that transcends all other realities: God, or The Holy." A historical event is not meaningful in and of itself, nor does it play a role in the formation of identity, until its meaning potential has been inferred and established. This potential must be transferred from the realm of chaotic contingency into an "orderly, meaningful, intelligible contingency." The fundamental construct that facilitates this transfer is *narration*, for narrative sets up the meaning structure that makes it possible for human beings to come to terms with historical contingency. *This is the form in which both the innermost human self and external events can be expressed.*[40]

If the resurrection was a historical event, even if it was without parallel, the need to express its meaning demanded its narration. Whatever the symbolic *value* of the resurrection, that is, however one might want to speak of its importance in analytical terms, the symbolic *content* is its narration. The narratives of the resurrection appearances of Jesus are the *what is* of the resurrection, while the explication is the *why so*.

In subsequent chapters, I hope to make the importance of all of this "history of history" very clear. At this point, I will summarize my selecting, collecting and presenting of these historical "facts" of historical scholarship by saying that I have attempted in *this* history writing to make the following points along the way. First, ancient history writing, which includes most of the writing in the New Testament, was in fact concerned with the correspondence of their narratives to actual events, including a predilection for such modern-sounding ingredients as coherence, consistency, and the testimony of eyewitnesses (Breisach, Momigliano, Burridge, et al.). Second, all historical investigations are undertaken within consciously or unconsciously held metaphysical and metanarrative considerations, seeking to create truly *historical* events from the past by placing them in meaning-producing

---

40. Schnelle, *Theology of the New Testament*, 29.

The History of History

narratives (White, Foucault, Barthes, et al.). And third, history writing is of greatest value when the narration of historical events is allowed to confront and challenge us by being inclusive of historical, structural, and ultimate dimensions of reality (McIntire, Cochrane Schnelle, et al.). This kind of history writing would represent—and the pun is deliberate—a *resurrection* of history.

Ultimately, we cannot responsibly say anything about the historicity of the resurrection of Jesus without knowing what we mean by history or historicity. Lacking any video, photographs, or even courtroom sketches of that first Easter morning, we are—in a material sense—reliant on written accounts of the resurrection appearances of Jesus. Knowing how historians have handled history writing throughout the centuries, and what kind of documents these are, should help us evaluate claims based on the examination of these documents by historians, theologians, and those integrative acrobats we call New Testament scholars, that the resurrection was or wasn't a historical event.

The Resurrection of History

QUESTIONS FOR CONSIDERATION

Seminary

1. Select a teaching of the church as an example. Can you identify whether this teaching reflects traditional, modern, or postmodern historical method?
2. Do you think the "third millennium" historical method is a step forward for theology or a step backward?

Study Group

1. What elements of the different kinds of history writing do you recognize from history classes, books, or lectures?
2. In what ways do you think it is important / not important to understand that "history" means different things at different times to different people?

Individual

1. When do you defer too quickly to "the church says . . ." and when do you too quickly defer to your own perspective?
2. When are you comfortable seeing yourself as shaped by the past and when are you uncomfortable?

4 The Theology of History

IN 1823, A YOUNG treasure hunter named Joseph Smith Jr. was praying alone in a wooded area, for the forgiveness of his sins. An angel named Moroni appeared to him and revealed to him the location of a set of buried golden plates, along with a breastplate and a set of stones whose reflective capabilities would allow him to interpret the ancient writing on the golden plates. For over four years, Smith returned to the location where the golden plates were buried, but the angel prevented him from removing them. Finally, in October of 1827, Smith returned with his then-expecting wife Emma, and was allowed to retrieve the plates, which he placed in a locked chest. The angel commanded him to not show the plates to anyone, but to translate them using the sacred stones. Smith had a sample of his translation from their reformed Egyptian characters authenticated by a prominent scholar, who later recanted his authentication when discovering their religious implications. Under pressure from an associate, Smith loaned the manuscript of the translation into that associate's keeping, who lost it; in punishment for losing the manuscript, the plates were taken from Smith by the angel for a time, but eventually given back to Smith. Smith recommenced his translating, and completed it in mid-year 1829, at which time he showed the plates to three associates, and later to male family members, who signed a declaration that they had seen the plates. The text produced was a religious history of the native American peoples: *The Book of Mormon* became one of the sacred scriptures of The Church of Jesus Christ of Latter Day Saints, popularly known as the Mormons.

What is intriguing for our purposes is that the first Mormons, including Smith himself, were careful to subject the revelation made to Smith to critical tests of history writing. As in traditionalist history writing (which the documents themselves were in the form of), they secured eyewitnesses to the existence of the golden plates. As in (the then emerging paradigm of) modern history writing, they subjected the characters and Smith's translation for independent verification. The authentication of the translation of the plates remains, for LDS scholars at least, a stubborn historical "fact" that must be taken into account when LDS claims to Smith's claims to prophetic status are being considered. While LDS faith is about much more than certain historical facts, there has always been an awareness that if the basic narrative is discounted, it undermines the remaining claims of the Church of Jesus Christ of Latter Day Saints, much as a crumbling foundation undermines the structural stability of a building.

Is that a reasonable view? Does religious faith really depend on historical events? Can it? Should it? What does that relationship of dependence look like? The discussion that follows involves some of biggest names in theology in the last century. Don't worry about memorizing their names, but rather enjoy the see-saw of ideas as each theologian in turn reacts to, borrows from, and builds on the ideas of others.

TROELTSCH'S DISTINCTION OF THEOLOGY FROM HISTORY

Ernst Troeltsch was a German Protestant theologian working in the latter half of the nineteenth century and the first quarter of the twentieth. Thoroughly modernist, he proposed reconceiving theology as the product of historical study, in the firm belief that historical study could ground Christianity as the ultimate "disclosure of divine reason."[1] Troeltsch identified two different methods of relating religious truths and historical considerations. Troeltsch labeled the deductive approach of deriving historical truths from theological axioms as "the dogmatic method," while he labeled the process of deriving theological truths from responsible historical inquiry as "the historical method." While both are internally consistent, and both have their difficulties, Troeltsch believed the historical method to be clearly superior. He insisted on keeping these methods separate. He especially deplored the last-minute rescue of problematic historical reconstructions by invoking divine intervention: "Should one admire the modesty of a theology that has come to the point of finding its ultimate foundation

---

1. Troeltsch, *Religion in History*, 27. The references here are taken from the opening essay in that anthology, "Historical Method and Dogmatic Method in Theology," written in 1898.

in a gap?"² Instead, he promoted the consistent application of a historical method containing three essential elements: the principle of criticism, the principle of analogy, and the principle of correlation.

The principle of *criticism* asserts that all historical events are subject to historical criticism. Since past events are only "historical" when agreed upon by historians, and historians are limited and fallible, the best that can be said of any historical event is that it has a *high degree* of certainty. If all historical events are only more or less *probable*, then all religious faith founded on historical events is also only more or less probably true. Troeltsch recognized that this conclusion would be problematic for those pious souls who crave certainty, but he maintained that religious maturity calls for embracing this ultimate uncertainty; just as a mature civilization builds upon the best knowledge it has at the time, so Christians are called to make do with the best historical knowledge they have of God's actions.

The principle of *analogy* asserts that "agreement with normal, customary, or at least frequently attested happenings and conditions as we have experienced them is the criterion of probability for all events that historical criticism can recognize as having actually or possibly happened."³ Troeltsch systematically refused to exempt events recorded in the scriptures on the premise of the divinely inspired nature of the Bible. He also was of the opinion that the calls for such exemptions were irrevocably waning, and that the only historical "facts" that might still call for exemption from this principle were "Jesus' moral character and the resurrection." These exemptions were permissible, Troeltsch believed, because historical method was capable of establishing that

> a God distinct from nature produced a personality superior to nature with eternally transcendent goals and the willpower to change the world . . . which to anyone sensitive enough to catch its echo in one's own soul, seems to be the conclusion of all previous religious movements and the starting point of a new phase in the history of religion, in which nothing [greater] yet has emerged.⁴

The principle of *correlation* asserts that only historical causes be identified to explain historical effects. Historical inquiry is impossible, and

---

2. Ibid., 31.

3. Ibid., 17.

4. Ibid., 27. Note that for Troeltsch, the "resurrection" referred to here is the mythologization of the impact that Jesus had on his followers. See Troeltsch, *Christian Religion* (originally published 1925), 219.

The Resurrection of History

history writing becomes ludicrous, when divine action is used to explain historical events. Troeltsch felt very strongly that it was just plain wrong to construct historical claims that implied that God's actions violated God's own ordained laws of nature. This would be tantamount to saying that God's establishing of the laws of nature was somehow flawed or incomplete, requiring patchwork solutions here and there. In Troeltsch's view, God had set the world in motion in a certain, necessary way. In the unfolding of history, "God is the universal consciousness, the reality in which all things exist, and the ground of values. In the history of religion, the idea of God gains increasing content, and the contribution of Christianity has been an outstanding one."[5]

It is rather obvious how Troeltsch's historical method discounts the orthodox understanding of the resurrection of Jesus. First, while the *accounts* of the resurrection of Jesus found in the New Testament might be suitably subject to historical criticism, the orthodox understanding has always been that *the fact of* the resurrection is designed to offer certainty of the theological implications of Jesus mission and message. Second, while the *idea* of resurrection might be part of our human experience, the *observation* of resurrection is not. Even if we experienced something apparently analogous to Jesus' resurrection, it would be categorically different, because it would not (according to the orthodox understanding) be the resurrection of the unique Son of God. Third, there is no serious suggestion that I know of that proposes a certain set of historical causes that can account for the historical resurrection of Jesus. In any case, if the resurrection of Jesus were *merely* a historical event, with no divine intervention, it would be a freak occurrence, but could not be called a "resurrection" with all the theological implications of that term (something we will discuss below).

Although Troeltsch believed himself to be championing a distinct historical method as the foundation of theology, it should be clear just how much theological content was already embedded in his "historical method." Troeltsch's historical method could only point to a certain kind of God, the kind envisioned by an immanent theism (which he seems to have borrowed from Hegel), in which God is seen as a progress-propelling principle within nature. This may not be the God of the Old and New Testaments, but Troeltsch would say that we have now, inspired by the example of Jesus of Nazareth, progressed beyond that limited vision. The kind of immanent theism upheld by Troeltsch is an attractive option for many in

---

5. MacQuarrie, *Twentieth-Century Religious Thought*, 143.

The Theology of History

our contemporary society, and would is for the better part consistent with the revisionist understanding of the resurrection of Jesus. The question that I would raise at this point is, would *Jesus* have recognized that image of God? If so, why do the New Testament writings depict him as perpetuating a soon-to-be-obsolete vision of a personal, intervening God? And if the Gospels have so grossly misconstrued Jesus' vision of God, how would we rely on them for any information about Jesus? On the other hand, if Jesus' vision of God was as the Gospels depict, doesn't that make him just another ancient prophet whose message is out of date? How would we, why would we, look to him for inspiration?

Martin Kahler responded not only to Troeltsch but to the idea that historical research could somehow ground us rationally in Christian faith. He argued that the only reliable records we have are those of the New Testament, especially the Gospels. It is true, of course, that the Gospels are not dispassionate, disinterested historical records, but rather the confessional documents of the early church proclaiming Jesus to be the unique Son of God. If on the one hand Jesus were simply a great man, analogous to other great men we might know, Kahler says, we have no record of him. If on the other hand Jesus were as unique as the Gospels depict, we have no theology-free historical method sufficient to analyze him. While Jesus may not be available to us as a *merely* historical figure, he is at least available to faith as a *historic* figure, one whose field of influence resounds through the centuries. Faith in Christ, according to Kahler, is not based on the historical credibility of the biblical record or the institutional credibility of the church, but on Christ's own credibility: "We want to make absolutely clear that ultimately we believe in Christ not on account of any authority, but because he himself evokes such faith from us. This thought that *Christ himself is the originator of the biblical picture of the Christ* is implicit in what was said earlier."[6]

Rudolf Bultmann, an existentialist New Testament scholar and theologian, was deeply affected by Kahler's challenge, but instead of agreeing with Kahler he responded by rigorously applying Troeltsch's principles of historical method to the Gospels with severe results. Applying the principle of criticism, he found the narratives of Jesus' life to be contradictory and deficient in internal chronology, external historical reference, and geography, and the words of Jesus to be stylized, formulaic, and unlikely to be supported by eyewitness accounts. Applying the principle of analogy, he found the stories of miraculous healings and nature miracles to be outside

---

6. Kahler, *So-Called Historical Jesus* (originally published 1897), 87.

the realm of that which could be considered as historical data. Applying the principle of correlation, he found more reason to attribute Jesus' words in the Gospels to the concerns of the early church than to a first-century Jewish rabbi, concluding that the Gospels were therefore largely attempts to re-historicize the original Christian proclamation.[7]

Bultmann concurred with Kahler that the Gospels don't allow us to reconstruct anything of the historical Jesus with any certainty, and that it is Kahler's *historic* Christ that counts for faith. He went further than Troeltsch or Kahler, however, saying that in any case the early Christian proclamation about Jesus, as the ministry of Paul proved, doesn't require any certain knowledge about the historical Jesus: "The Christ of the kerygma is not a historical figure which could enjoy continuity with the historical Jesus. The kerygma which proclaims him is a historical phenomenon, however."[8] Taking his cue from the philosophy of Martin Heidegger,[9] Bultmann relocated the ground for Christian faith from the past and placed it entirely in the present, with faith in God's call as its own justification.

Karl Barth was a Swiss theologian best known for his voluminous *Church Dogmatics*. Barth's approach to historical understanding is emblematic of his entire approach to theology. Barth was deeply affected by the rise of Communism, Fascism, and National Socialism, all of which in one way or another laid claim to supremacy and ultimate allegiance, the kind of allegiance that a Christian, in Barth's opinion, should only owe to God. Barth was adamant that only *God* was God, and that God's *self*-revelation, rather than our attempts to "peek behind the curtain" and discern the hidden deity, was the proper subject matter of theology.

Barth challenged Bultmann's rejection of historical fact as ingredient to Christian faith, claiming that the original kerygma contained at least two essential historical assertions, that Jesus died and that Jesus was raised. Barth denied that theological statements should be made subject to the critique of human understanding, because that would overrule God's freedom to introduce anything truly new to us. He pointed out that all highly unusual events—even if actually historical—could be excluded by overzealous application of the historical method, and that the historical method was therefore no sure route to historical truth. He also questioned whether or

---

7. Bultmann, *History of the Synoptic Tradition* (originally published 1926); Bultmann, *Jesus and the Word*; and Ogden, *New Testament and Theology*.

8. Bultmann, "Primitive Christian Kerygma and the Historical Jesus," 17–18.

9. Cf. Heidegger, *Being and Time* (originally published 1927).

not our present categories, whether they be anthropological or historical or scientific, should be given the ultimate authority to arbitrate theological truth: something such as the resurrection would be, Barth admitted, astounding in the categories of *any* age, but that doesn't make it untrue or unreal.

Into the mid-twentieth century, other scholars such as Hans Cönzlemann, Joachim Jeremias, Heinrich Ott, and Ernst Käsemann wanted to find a middle ground between accepting the New Testament as unvarnished historical data on the one hand and despairing of finding any historical truth about Jesus on the other.[10] H. Richard Niebuhr helpfully suggested that we remember that history writing about any religious phenomena will be colored by whether or not one is committed to membership in that religious group, but insisted that faith-commitment alone does not necessarily make the claims of historical truth invalid.[11] Van Harvey, on the other hand, flatly rejected Niebuhr's olive branch, saying, "When faith is used as a justification for believing historical claims that otherwise could not be justified by our normal warrants and backings, the machinery of rational assessment comes to a shuddering halt."[12] If historical claims are not publicly accessible, they are ultimately dogmatic rather than rationally arrived at. Instead, Harvey suggested, we should allow the image of Jesus that emerges from the faith-claim that he was resurrected by God to challenge and confirm our faith.[13]

THE REJOINING OF THEOLOGY AND HISTORY: PANNENBERG, MOLTMANN, BALTHASAR

In the second half of the twentieth century, three theologians stood out among the rest in wrestling with the relationship of theology and history in

---

10. Cönzelmann, "Method of the Life-of-Jesus Research," 68; Jeremias, *Problem of the Historical Jesus*, 10–11; Ott, "Historical Jesus and the Ontology of History," 170; and Käsemann, *Essays on New Testament Themes*, 46.

11. H. Richard Niebuhr, *Meaning of Revelation*. Terrence W. Tilley points out, however, that Niebuhr's logic might not apply as well to the resurrection of Jesus as to the exodus, which Niebuhr uses as his paradigm, because in the case of the resurrection we are not simply interpreting what can be observed from different perspectives, but we are also engaging the question of whether or not the purported event is even possible. Cf. Tilley, *History, Theology, and Faith*, 22–25.

12. Harvey, *Historian and the Believer*, 46.

13. Ibid., 281.

regards to the resurrection of Jesus. Each of these in turn weave theology and history more closely together, in some ways paralleling the movement among historians traced in the previous chapter. Wolfhart Panneberg might be the best known among evangelical Protestants, holding historical fact in high regard. Jürgen Moltmann might be the best known among mainline Protestants, having connected Christian eschatology (faith's vision of the future) to social justice, ecology, and other forms of political engagement. Hans Urs von Balthasar might be the best known to Catholics, having greatly influenced the thinking of John Paul II and Benedict XVI.

Pannenberg understood that twentieth-century historians necessarily approached ancient texts with a different "horizon" of thought. Instead of simply imposing his or her own preconceptions on an ancient text, the open-minded historian should be free to allow the text to widen his or her horizon, making it possible to go beyond the limits of their preconceptions in an act of scholarly creativity. Since the future of humanity has already been revealed in Jesus Christ, what the historian encounters in reading the New Testament is not simply testimony regarding the past but testimony regarding the future. Troeltsch and even as great a figure as Hegel missed this point, Pannenberg says, because of the poor state of biblical scholarship in their day: "The eschatological character of the message of Jesus was beyond [Hegel] as it was beyond the New Testament interpreters of the time."[14] Pannenberg, like Barth, emphasizes the self-revelation of God in history, but God's involvement in human history is only known from the *end* of history, which was revealed *proleptically*—that is, with the end of history revealed in, or even inserted into, the middle of history—in the death and resurrection of Jesus. This appreciation of Jesus as the end of history was historically prepared by the forward-looking faith of the Jewish people. Jesus' stated mission, the inauguration of the reign of God, was vindicated in the resurrection, and the church's faith was built on this vindication, such that "an event that is expressible only in the language of the resurrection is to be asserted as a historical occurrence."[15]

Pannenberg asserts that, on the historical evidence alone, the originally independent resurrection traditions of the empty tomb, taken together with the record of appearances listed by Paul, suggest a high degree of historical probability, which is all that historical inquiry on its own can produce. He rejects, however, the exclusion of the resurrection on the grounds

---

14. Pannenberg, "Hermeneutics and Universal History," 151.
15. Pannenberg, *Jesus—God and Man*, 32.

that it violates natural or scientific "laws," because our understanding of such laws are always partial and evolving:

> As long as historiography does not begin dogmatically with a narrow concept of reality according to which "dead men do not rise," it is not clear why historiography should not in principle be able to speak about Jesus' resurrection as the explanation that is best established by such events as the disciples' experiences of the appearances and the discovery of the empty tomb.[16]

Pannenberg admits that Christians acting as historians may have to claim an exemption from the dominant preconceptions among historians, but for Pannenberg this represents an exemption based on historical evidence itself. Ted Peters applauds Pannenberg's move here, saying that he is employing Troeltsch's principle of analogy *positively*, allowing into evidence those events which are *like* events we have already experienced, rather than using the principle of analogy *negatively*, by excluding all events that are not *identical in kind* to events we have already experienced.[17]

Jürgen Moltmann agrees with Pannenberg that the world is best conceived of as an open system, where events are not simply manifestations of some static, eternal truth, but may be meaningful in themselves. As a *Christian* theologian Moltmann says that he must take seriously the history of Israel as uniquely revealing of God's eschatological intentions.[18] The resurrection of Jesus is not an historical event in the usual sense because the conditions for its occurrence were not already present in historical processes. Although it occurred within history, the resurrection cannot be defined by our standard definition of history. Moltmann says that "Christ's death and resurrection are not two happenings belonging to the same category. . . . Christ's death on the cross is an historical fact—Christ's resurrection is an apocalyptic happening."[19] By this Moltmann doesn't mean that the resurrection did not happen in history or that it cannot be considered as

---

16. Ibid., 109.

17. Peters, "Shorter Communications," 477. In fact, Peter's point is easily seen without invoking divine causation by creating a fictional scenario wherein civilization as we know it collapses and humankind reverts to bronze-age technology for ten thousand years. If a document is discovered ten millennia from now that describes an ancient phenomena called "television," it would be without analogy in the future historian's experience—but that does not mean that television never existed. In this case, negative application of the principle of analogy would lead to a false historical conclusion.

18. Moltmann, *Theology of Hope*, 141.

19. Moltmann, *Way of Jesus*, 214.

The Resurrection of History

a historical event. What he does mean is that while death is graspable by historians as a historical event, the resurrection cannot be understood for what it is by historical categories alone, but requires theological appreciation of its historicity to be understood for what it is.

For Moltmann, expanding the concept of history as Pannenberg does is not enough to grasp the resurrection as a historical event; one must also commit oneself to engage in the existential questions it raises. Historical reconstruction is always done in partnership with historical interpretation: there are no *uninterpreted* historical facts. While the Gospel accounts of the resurrection may amount to "relatively well-attested historical facts," it is "impossible to filter out the substance of these experiences in the form of naked facts detached from their subjective human interpretation."[20] The witnesses to the resurrection were testifying to an objective historical event, but only by comprehending it as messianic and eschatological: without understanding something of its ultimate significance, they would not have spoken of it as resurrection. A Christian theologian cannot authentically speak of the historical event of the resurrection of Jesus without bringing theological interpretation to bear.

Hans Urs von Balthasar even more explicitly rejects the notion that there is any such thing as a purely *a posteriori* approach to God's revelation, as if theology could spring from historical study: "Historical science may attempt to be neutral as regards the philosophy of history, but it cannot controvert the fact that its subject—man in his acts and sufferings—conducts himself, in small things and great, according to his basic idea of ultimate meaning, that is to say, as a philosopher."[21] Theology may be the interpretation of divine revelation, but God—and here Balthasar echoes Barth—is self-interpreted in history. Balthasar calls this self-interpretation "Theo-drama," meaning to indicate the freedom with which God chooses times and places to involve others in the unfolding of human destiny. Seeing history as the stage of this Theo-drama, the theologian refuses to mark off separate spheres in which the theologian and the historian can work in parallel fashion, because there is no historical reality that is out of bounds for the theologian: "The refusal of any such agreed demarcation on the part of theology, though it may look like and be called arrogance, is really no more than respect for the methodological demands of its subject."[22] History

---

20. Moltmann, "Resurrection of Christ," 74–75.
21. Balthasar, *Word and Revelation*, 32.
22. Balthasar, *Theology of History*, 18.

and theology always work together, and work together better when they acknowledge that they are working together.

The uniqueness of Jesus and his resurrection causes no embarrassment for Balthasar. The uniqueness of Jesus, both in theology and in history, subordinates all other modes and categories. Jesus is not held up against other norms, but is in himself *the* norm of history: "The Son's action is what history is for."[23] The recognition of God's action transforms all other historical observations; where faith is absent, there is often the tendency to concentrate on "the secondary, time-bound elements" which, if they are elevated to primary status, cause the whole picture to be distorted. This "transposition" of theological appreciation into historical inquiry is to be judged on its ability to reveal God's intentions, and not on how neatly the theological appreciation fits into non-theological categories. The virgin birth, for instance, must remain uniquely outside all other categories, because it is unique within human history. Sometimes, says Balthasar, the lack of analogy is exactly what needs to be preserved.[24]

Balthasar's theological understanding of history is not that history somehow exemplifies non-historical, eternal truths, but rather that history is where God's eternal intentions become reality: God is revealed in "the real, lived history of a real man," and "the Passion is a true drama where something of soteriological significance is genuinely accomplished."[25] Similarly, the historicity of the resurrection is absolutely vital to the conception of history as Theo-drama:

> Establishing that the all-controlling turning point occurred on a prespecified day shows that this turning point was strictly provided for, and also able to be substantiated by witnesses, just like everything else that happened in Jesus' mortal life. The dating here is just as important as that of the Passion under Pontius Pilate. The point in time at which Jesus' new, deathless life takes its departure from our mortal history is no sometime or other, but a now that can be established for this history, which continues to unfold afterward.[26]

---

23. Ibid., 65.
24. Balthasar, *Theo-Drama: Theological Dramatic Theory*, 2:96ff.
25. Chapp, "Revelation," 20.
26. Balthasar, *Credo*, 57.

As if to underline once and for all that history is not an awkward, uncertain "remainder" in an otherwise timeless theological system, Balthasar says bluntly: "History is itself the system in Christianity."[27]

TROELTSCH'S PRINCIPLES REVISITED

The contributions of Pannenberg, Moltmann, and Balthasar are the product of the dialectical, back-and-forth, theological conversation of the century preceding them. While they may seem like rather finely tuned abstractions, they prove quite useful when examining contemporary arguments regarding the resurrection of Jesus. Even though eminent theologians such as Pannenberg, Moltmann, and Balthasar have highlighted the limitations of the applications of Troeltsch's three principles in history writing, old habits die hard.

Michael Martin employs the principle of criticism when he argues that (1) the resurrection of Jesus is improbable relative to our background knowledge, and (2) the evidence for it is weak, so (3) therefore the claim that Jesus was resurrected should be disbelieved.[28] In doing so, he is echoing the eighteenth-century argument of David Hume about all miracles. Hume asserted that since historical claims are about probabilities, and since it is always less probable that a violation of nature's laws has taken place than that it has, all historical claims about miracles should be disbelieved. This shifting of the burden of proof to those who would believe in miracles is part of the modern paradigm of history, which still has its contemporary advocates. Sarah Coakley more recently commented on Hume's argument, saying that while we cannot necessarily rule out a violation of cosmological law, the burden of proof must be on anyone claiming a miracle has occurred.[29]

Richard Swinburne counters that Hume's "mistake was to suppose that the only relevant background theory to be established from wider evidence was a scientific theory about what are the laws of nature."[30] If there is evidence, says Swinburne, to believe in the kind of God who may freely suspend the laws of nature, then the reality of God has to be taken into account every bit as much as the reality of cosmological laws. In fact, the

---

27. Balthasar, *Theology of Karl Barth*, 340.
28. Martin, "Resurrection as Initially Improbable," 46.
29. Coakley, "Is the Resurrection a Historical Event?," 93.
30. Swinburne, *Resurrection of God Incarnate*, 25.

The Theology of History

reporting of a miracle is most likely due to the perception that a violation of cosmological law has in fact taken place, because that's what makes the event noteworthy. Instead, to be fair, the evidence for or against the historicity of the resurrection of Jesus must be weighed in the context of explicitly stipulated background theory, including both theological and scientific suppositions.

Robert Greg Cavin uses the principle of analogy to argue that the accounts of the resurrection of Jesus do not provide us with sufficient information about the "the dispositional properties" of the resurrected Jesus (e.g., immortality, insusceptibility to aging, etc.) to determine whether or not the resurrection of Jesus bears any analogy to our own experience. The resurrection, therefore, says Cavin, cannot be evaluated and therefore not substantiated in historical terms. Any historical claims about unicorns would face a similar fate, we could say, because we do not know anything about unicorns to be able to judge the likelihood of a claim about them.

It can be quickly countered, however, that the goal of historical inquiry is to understand historical events on their own terms, that is, in the understanding of those reporting. In the case of the resurrection what is being reported is that something occurred which was actually and categorically new: "Science knows only the matter of this world but it cannot forbid theology to believe that God is capable of bringing about something totally new."[31] It is relatively easy to slip into *positivism*, where we project the interpretive schema of the current scientific consensus—which is what "laws" of nature really are—onto the world we are observing, and run the risk of excluding observations, including historical accounts, that would challenge that understanding. Cosmological categories have changed in the past and will change again, based on observations that run counter to accepted theory. Remembering this prevents us from presumptuously precluding well-attested observations. Allowing for such challenges could conceivably advance our theological or even our scientific knowledge.

Geza Vermes uses the principle of correlation to argue that the New Testament accounts intended to report a spiritual rather than a bodily resurrection. After careful analysis, Vermes deems that historical reasoning would have to reject any scenario in which (a) the body of Jesus was removed by anyone, (b) the disciples mistook an empty tomb for the tomb of Jesus, or (c) Jesus somehow survived crucifixion. Vermes therefore declares the reports of an empty tomb to be symbolically and not literally

---

31. Polkinghorne, *Science and Theology*, 115–16.

The Resurrection of History

intended—*because divine causation must be methodologically excluded from historical inquiry*.

This would naturally cause anyone entertaining the orthodox view of the resurrection to ask why, if a "spiritual" rather than a bodily resurrection was what the early Christians believed and intended to communicate, did they invent the stories of the empty tomb? And, one would have to ask why did they not coordinate their stories better than they did? William Lane Craig rightly points out that "an apologetic intention may sometimes tell us why an evangelist *includes* an incident, not why he *invents* an incident."[32] To rule out divine activity in considering the historicity of the Gospel accounts of the resurrection would entail having to dismiss the intelligibility and/or historicity of nearly all that Jesus is purported to have said and done. To do so would be to *presuppose* a theological cosmology in which the historical accounts of Jesus' ministry as well as his resurrection could not be entered into evidence.

Terrence W. Tilley struggles, on the other hand, to establish some kind of accord between theologians and historians by differentiating between "event" and "action":

> The testimony at the root of the Christian tradition does not claim that an event has occurred, but that God has acted. The resurrection is not *merely* an event. It is fundamentally, and more significantly, an action. The agent is God. The *result* is that Jesus is exalted and glorified. . . . *That* is of interest, if not to social historians, then to theologians. Historians properly write of human actions and events. They may attempt to infer what the agents' intentions were in performing specific acts. But while events are within their scope, acts of God are beyond the pale of properly historical research.[33]

What Tilley says here is true, but we should exercise caution. While it may be beyond the scope of a historian to declare a historical event to be an act of God without becoming a theologian, a historian should not be obliged to declare an event to be unhistorical simply because there is no better explanation for it than that it was in fact an act of God. Furthermore, while it may be beyond the scope of a theologian to declare an act of God (e.g., the virgin birth of Jesus) to be a historical event, neither should

---

32. Craig, *Assessing the New Testament Evidence*, 177.
33. Tilley, *History, Theology, and Faith*, 52–53.

a theologian declare an event to be beyond God's power to enact simply because existing historical categories are inadequate to it.

As we have seen, there is no universal agreement among either secular historians about exactly what history writing is or how it should be conducted, but there is an emerging consensus that history writing must take into account, in the first place, the perspectives and worldviews of those that are being written about and, in the second place, the perspectives of those that are being written for. Both of these are becoming increasingly difficult to maintain in a world where the mixing of populations, the proliferation of media, and the ubiquity of the internet means that there is no "safe" audience and nothing that is "safely" presumed. This is felt in the academy, but it is also increasingly felt in political circles, in religious communities, and in friendly chats among neighbors. Especially in the West, where the freedom to be wrong is cherished alongside the ability to be right, the need to preface all inquiry with a long list of assumptions can become an onerous task—but woe to whomever neglects it!

Theologians, it should be said, also face similar challenges. It might appear to those specializing in other disciplines that Christian theologians should have it easier, since they are all of (basically) one mind, but that is far from the case. The fantasy of so many theologians all in the same boat pulling on the oars at the same time is quickly dispelled by the multiplicity of Orthodox, Protestant, and Catholic traditions and sub-traditions. The larger Christian tradition is twenty centuries in the making, and in many ways reliant on the Jewish tradition that adds another fifteen centuries to its intellectual and spiritual lineage. The reality is that Christian theology has been undertaken in so many different languages in different social contexts that terminology and labels are often lost in translation from one culture to another and/or one era to another. Theologians may be excused for thinking that history writing is a relatively unified and unproblematic discipline!

Both historians and theologians also face the difficulties inherent in their separate specializations. Both historians and theologians can focus narrowly on one subject or one era, and have relatively little knowledge of larger systems and movements. Very few historians actually feel themselves competent to discuss the principles of history writing (historiography), and very few theologians feel themselves competent to discuss the theology of history. Knowledge of theology on the part of historians is often rather basic, as is the historical knowledge of theologians. Given the present academic climate that suggests anyone presuming encyclopedic knowledge is self-deceived, this situation is unlikely to change very soon. My present investigation, therefore, needs to move ahead with all modesty, and with eagerness at the prospect of being properly "schooled" by both historians and theologians.

Before moving on from here, let me declare where *I* emerge from the above discussion. As someone who once upon a time studied metaphysics and epistemology, I concur with Tilley when he says that the Troeltschian axioms "are only rules of thumb necessary for engaging in the practice of doing history, descriptions of the common sense of the discipline of history, not philosophical foundations of the practice or metaphysical necessities."[34] As an amateur historian, I concur with Pannenberg that the event of the resurrection is accessible to historians who do not irrationally preclude it. As a student of theology, I concur with Moltmann that we fundamentally misunderstand the testimony of the New Testament if we do not appreciate that the resurrection of Jesus is depicted as an eschatological event within history. As a Christian with particular faith-commitments, I concur with Balthasar that the resurrection of Jesus is not merely a demonstration of eternal truth but that history is the theatre in which God's activity is played out. And as an eternal optimist, I concur with the disposition of any historian or theologian who does not *preclude* the potential insights of the other. We need to keep searching for a way for historians and theologians to work together rather than mutually exclusive silos, and the resurrection of Jesus may well be the single best test-case to explore new avenues of rapprochement.

---

34. Ibid., 43.

QUESTIONS FOR CONSIDERATION

Seminary

1. What is your assessment of the accounts of miracles in the New Testament narratives?
2. How do you react to Balthasar's contention that in Christianity, "history is the system"?

Study Group

1. Are there any universal assumptions that we can make about history or humankind?
2. Are there any beliefs that need to be held in order for someone to be legitimately called a Christian?

Individual

1. What doubts have been created or erased so far as you've read this book?
2. When do you ever feel angry toward those who attack what you believe?

5   The Employment of History

As a Christian preacher for more than a quarter century, I was an amateur historian. Every preacher is. In preparation for my sermons, I would read several commentaries on the selected preaching text. Week after week I would find myself tripping over scholarly pronouncements on what Jesus really did or did not say, what Jesus really did or did not do, what Jesus really did or did not mean. And week after week I found myself constantly saying, "Yeah, but . . ." It's not that I needed or even wanted to disagree with their conclusions; many of them would have proved much easier to offer up than what I was thinking. I was always puzzled, though, at how assured the commentators were, despite their varying points of view, and how seldom I could find any identification of the commentator's own positions or assumptions, as if the commentator had found that intellectual sweet spot of absolute objectivity.

On top of those weekly struggles, I would frequently have one or another of my very literate and well-educated local hearers hand me a book on a theological topic by some popular writer or other, and usually the gift would be accompanied by an appreciative comment such as, "I like what she has to say," or, "I agree with what he writes." It was almost always the case that I sadly noted that the appreciative comments seemed to be more an indication of what the reader *wanted* to be true, rather than the conclusion of any long and labored reflection. Most of the time I knew that the eager reader did not have the critical tools with which to question the author's assumptions, methods, or conclusions. And then I realized that neither did I. I recall sitting down with two professors at the Toronto School of Theology who were screening applicants for admission to doctoral studies there, who asked me what my burning questions were. I replied that my concerns were rather basic: I wanted to know if all that stuff in the Gospels was *true*. I was

The Employment of History

greeted with friendly but puzzled looks, and a few more probing questions. When in some context or other the word "apologetics" tumbled out of my mouth, there were broad smiles of recognition. They didn't teach apologetics there, but they would see what they could do.

If you're not familiar with the term, "apologetics" comes from the Greek word *apologia*, and in English would be better translated as "defense" rather than "apology," as apologetics have nothing to do with taking the blame for anything. I suppose that my studies did take on an apologetic character, and my thesis certainly wound up being somewhat apologetic in nature. I did not, however, as others have, attempt to *prove* the historicity of the resurrection of Jesus—that it actually happened—but I did want to know if the resurrection of Jesus could be legitimately considered to be a historical event. I worked forward and backward from this question, backward into the larger assumptions about what history writing is and what it entails, and forward into what the theological and social implications of asserting its historicity would be—*if* it were in fact historical. In the end, I like to think that I was prepared for either a positive or negative answer, but I confess to you at this point that, having noted some of the ups, downs, and sideways-drifts of Western culture, I am not inclined to automatically believe that whatever is current thinking about an issue is necessarily best just because it is the latest. I fully realize that what *I* find satisfying might not be what *you* will find satisfying when all is said and done, but I hope my brief look at New Testament scholars in this chapter will highlight some of the issues that any thoughtful reader of the New Testament needs to wrestle with.

THE QUESTS FOR THE HISTORICAL JESUS

New Testament scholarship is an interdisciplinary enterprise that involves linguistic studies, literary criticism, history, archaeology, anthropology, and theology. New Testament scholars are expected to be thoroughly acquainted with the social and political context of the Near East in the first century, and be conversant in the opinions of other New Testament scholars, past and present. It is unreasonable to expect complete mastery of all these facets and disciplines, and most New Testament scholars have their individual emphases and specialties. A history of New Testament scholarship in the West is often depicted in the form of three "quests" for the historical truth behind the theologically charged depictions of Jesus in the New Testament.

The Resurrection of History

The origins of the so-called First Quest for the Historical Jesus can be traced to the late eighteenth century. While most biblical scholarship at that time was dedicated to apologetic tasks such as harmonizing the chronological and geographical references in the Gospels, Samuel Reimarus was systematically dissecting the accounts of the miraculous in scripture, and concluding that, as far as the Gospels were concerned,

> Jesus taught some of the principles of sound (i.e., natural) religion, but this is peripheral to the *actual* meaning of the gospel story, a tissue of lies on Jesus' part and lies by his disciples. Not only exegetically but also hermeneutically, this constituted a precise reversal of practically everyone else's view, from right to left.[1]

This separation of "the historical Jesus" from the biblical narratives that claims to describe his life came to full flower in 1835 in D. F. Strauss's *The Life of Jesus Critically Examined* that viewed the historical Jesus as "a hidden figure, buried under layers of theological tradition and debate."[2] Strauss concluded that every miracle reported in the Gospels was actually a myth created to reinforce the proclamation of the early church and bolster conviction that Jesus was the long-prophesied messiah, or an exaggeration of some less impressive event for the end of fanning the flames of religious enthusiasm.

While Strauss's opinions created a firestorm in the academy, it was Ernst Renan, a Frenchman, who popularized this critical approach in his bestselling *Life of Jesus* in 1860.[3] Renan's approach was not to attack the Gospels but to approach them critically as one would any other historical source. In doing so he freely rejected their miraculous elements, and tried to peel away the theological developments to get to the real Jesus who, in Renan's reckoning, was a noble figure proclaiming an immanent kingdom to all those who would have "ears to hear." This separation of the *real* Jesus from the theologically constructed figure depicted in the Gospels was taken up into the theology of Schleiermacher, Ritschl, and other representatives of the new theological "liberalism." The First Quest came to a screeching halt with Albert Schweitzer's *The Quest of the Historical Jesus*.[4] Schweitzer accused these scholars of projecting their own assumptions into the mind of Jesus, in order to re-create him in their own image. Just because *we* don't

---

1. Frei, *Eclipse of the Biblical Narrative*, 114.
2. Bray, *Biblical Interpretation Past and Present*, 332.
3. Renan, *Life of Jesus* (originally published 1860).
4. Schweitzer, *Quest of the Historical Jesus* (originally published 1910).

believe in miracles, or the coming apocalypse, Schweitzer reminded us, doesn't mean that Jesus didn't. Removing our assumptions of what Jesus *must have* believed, a more natural reading of the Gospels finds that Jesus was an apocalyptic prophet, and perhaps one whose mission ended in tragic but noble failure.

The beginning of the so-called Second Quest for the Historical Jesus can arguably be traced back to Ersnt Käsemann in the mid-twentieth century, who sought to balance skepticism for the claims of the Gospels with the need to somehow connect the early Christian proclamation to the historical Jesus. After all, the Gospels *only and always* depict Jesus as the "Lord of the community which believes in him," and fail to offer a convincing portrait of Jesus, for

> as soon as he is portrayed as speaking and acting, this human course becomes an unbroken series of divine revelations and mighty acts, which has no common basis of comparison with any other human life and thus can no longer be comprehended within the category of the historical.[5]

For Käsemann, the parables may offer some reliable evidence as to what Jesus really said or who Jesus really was, but even these are so formulaic as to be problematic. The only material from the Gospels we can be reasonably sure represent the historical Jesus are those pieces which would be ill-fitting in *either* first-century Judaism *or* the early church, which was dominated in the first decades by Jewish Christians. One such set of sayings, Käsemann conjectured, is the set where Jesus claims to supersede Moses' authority ("But I say to you . . ."). Käsemann did acknowledge, having heard Schweitzer's argument, that miracles were not out of bounds for first-century historians as they are for us, but rejected any reports of the miraculous from our *historical* consideration. In the end, he called on his readers to join him in clinging to the "pitiful threads" of genuine historical knowledge of the real Jesus rather than let their imaginations run utterly wild.

James M. Robinson, Burton Mack, and others involved in the later development of the "Jesus Seminar" similarly rejected the Gospels' accounts of Jesus' miracles. To get to the historical Jesus, we must examine the credibility of what the Gospels report Jesus to have said. Well into the twenty-first century, many scholars continue the Jesus Seminar's tradition of privileging the sayings of Jesus in the Gospels for historical purposes,

---

5. Käsemann, *Essays on New Testament Themes*, 19.

rating them along a four-point scale from authentic to inauthentic. As Mark Allen Powell observes, "Most of the New Questers required even greater evidence of certainty for what they affirmed than would usually be expected for historical research in the secular academy."[6] With such conditions, and so little surviving evidence, it is not surprising that the Second Quest resulted in little but conjectures of what Jesus might have or must have said. Many suppose, however, that these scholars go too far, delivering their conclusions with far too much certainty built on too little evidence. In the end, many of them fall back into the same trap as First Questers, re-creating the historical Jesus in a manner that reflects more of their own likes and dislikes than anything else.

The so-called Third Quest for the Historical Jesus is in most respects a more optimistic affair. These scholars reckon that, given the willingness of members of the early church to endure persecution and even martyrdom for the sake of being identified with Jesus, it is likely that the early church's production of the Gospels was at the very least a *good faith* effort to connect their proclamation with the historical Jesus. Consequently, the scholars of the Third Quest seek to neither privilege nor completely discount the Gospels as historical sources, but use them alongside other sources for understanding the circumstances and life of Jesus. The Third Quest seeks to ground Jesus not in the theological or philosophical presuppositions of our time but rather in what we independently know of Jesus' time. Jesus' beliefs about himself are taken seriously, even if there is a critical process whereby the reliability of sayings attributed to Jesus is still in play. The miracles of Jesus are not rejected *in toto*, but rather taken individually and assessed against the backdrop of a day and age when healing miracles were deemed to be part of how in fact some elements of the world worked. Messianic expectation is understood as part of the cultural fabric in first-century Judaism, from which Jesus' sense of himself and his mission arose.

The New Testament scholars we will discuss below are for the most part scholars of the Third Quest, broadly conceived, aware to at least some degree of the issues we have raised in the first part of this book. We will consider these scholars in three groups: those who seek to *insulate* theological concerns from historical research, those who seek to *critique* theological concerns with historical research, and those who seek to *integrate* theological concerns and historical research. It would be unfair to say that any one, let alone all, of the scholars treated below fit perfectly into these

---

6. Powell, *Jesus as a Figure in History*, 22.

categories. The object here is to observe the variety of ways in which New Testament scholars employ their implicit or explicit historical method as they deal with the resurrection of Jesus.

INSULATING THEOLOGICAL CONCERNS FROM HISTORICAL RESEARCH

Some recent New Testament scholars seek to insulate theological concerns from historical research. They don't necessarily think their theological concerns are vulnerable to attack, but rather they see theology and history as two separate disciplines that can and perhaps should function independently when it comes to consideration of the resurrection of Jesus.

William Lane Craig claims to be able to demonstrate the historical credibility of the resurrection of Jesus without reference to theology. Craig longs nostalgically for the pre-critical days when the Gospels were on an equal footing with other historical sources, a situation "supplanted in the nineteenth century by an inwardly-oriented apologetic through the advance in biblical criticism and the tide of subjectivism which swept Europe."[7] Craig reconstructs how a historical argument for the resurrection might look today: (1) setting aside historical skepticism; (2) defending the possibility of miracles; and (3) weighing the evidence of the empty tomb, the appearances of the risen Jesus, and the origin of the Christian Way (including dissimilarity with Judaism).[8] Fleshing out some of the elements of that argument, Craig complains that the Gospel accounts are often treated unfairly as historical evidence, but in doing so he seems to close his eyes to their obviously apologetic agenda. Craig treats the resurrection appearances—which were relatively "private," involving only previously committed disciples—as identical in their value as historical evidence: "I would go so far as to say that there is not a single event in the resurrection narratives that is not *in principle* historically verifiable or falsifiable."[9]

Craig asks the historian to be open-minded toward the possibility of miracles, wherein a cause *outside* of history effects an event *within* history, but he nowhere admits his theological motivation. As a committed Christian, Craig has no interest in Jesus simply surviving crucifixion or being somehow naturally revived. For Craig, as for others, Jesus' postmortem

---

7. Craig, *Historical Argument for the Resurrection*, 475.
8. Ibid., 544–46.
9. Ibid., 419.

appearances would merely be a historical oddity without religious significance if God did not raise Jesus. Craig seems to lack Panneberg's or Swinburne's awareness that another "background theory," namely biblical theism, must be introduced at this point in order to make sense of what the New Testament documents report. In my view, ultimately Craig insulates theological concerns from historical research in a manner that leaves him without any way in which to label the postmortem appearances of Jesus as "resurrection."

Gary R. Habermas likewise attempts to make a historical case for the resurrection of Jesus that is free of theological argument.[10] Habermas's principle strategy is to minimize the influence of his own subjectivity by enlisting the greatest possible number of ancient testimonies and references to the existence and resurrection of Jesus. While he is willing to point out the effect of subjectivity on the modern historian in reading the Gospels, Habermas does not apply the same criticism to the Gospel writers. He displays no knowledge of source or redaction criticism (investigations of how each Gospel writer selected and assembled existing material), and makes no argument for or about their reliability as historical sources. He quotes from sources as diverse as 1 John, Philippians, and 2 Timothy, without any indication that their authorship might affect their value as historical evidence. Habermas nowhere even entertains the possibility that the Gospel accounts of the empty tomb are pious fictions meant to metaphorize the early Christian experience that Jesus was alive despite the popularity of that view among scholars.

Habermas treats his compiled texts in a manner that could be characterized as *historically empiricist*, in which ancient sources are treated as brute facts, which themselves are able to make the case for the resurrection of Jesus without qualification or interpretation. Like Craig, Habermas calls for an open mind in regard to miraculous events such as the resurrection without naming the elements of any background theory that would allow for something like the resurrection of Jesus to have occurred. His selection and organization of texts is clearly guided by familiar theological suppositions, including the infallibility and consequent historical reliability of scripture. Habermas declares the resurrection to be without *natural analogy*, thereby requiring him to appeal to divine causation, even though he contends that he has built an argument for the resurrection of Jesus exclusive of theological considerations. In my view, Habermas's "argument"

---

10. Habermas, *Ancient Evidence of the Life of Jesus*.

insulates theological concerns from historical research by ignoring all recognizable historical method.

Pheme Perkins takes a very different route in insulating theological concerns from historical research, dealing with the New Testament not as historical narratives but as primarily reflective of the theological declarations of the first-century Christians.[11] Perkins works in a structuralist mode that considers the relationship of individual texts to the theological web they are meant to support, but seldom if ever employing those texts to "recover a way into the reality of that earlier world of discourse."[12] Perkins adopts as her starting point a series of theological claims from Hans Kung:

> 1. Resurrection cannot be described as a historical event in the ordinary sense of the word.... 2. Speaking of resurrection as an "eschatological event" distinguished it from miraculous intervention in the natural order, such as the revival of a corpse or a near-death experience. It also implies that resurrection is an event for Jesus, not merely a change of awareness on the part of the disciples.... 3. The variety of traditions and types of witnesses make it impossible to reduce resurrection to the projection of the disciples' need to recover the "heady intimacy" of their fellowship with Jesus.... Finally, "eschatological event" implies that the "bodily" reality involved is discontinuous with the material reality we experience.[13]

Perkins doesn't say that the New Testament texts are without historical reference, but she is extremely cautious when it comes to historical reconstruction of the resurrection event, saying only that "the combination of an early tradition of appearances of the Lord and the conviction that Jesus' tomb was empty would help to explain the significance of the resurrection in the Christian message about Jesus."[14]

Perkins admits that the New Testament narratives of the empty tomb show "little elaboration of miraculous detail" in comparison with later apocryphal stories, but in the end "the gospels tell us much less about the historical events surrounding the resurrection than they do about the legacy of faith in Jesus as the risen One that has shaped the traditions that have

---

11. Perkins, *Resurrection: New Testament Witness and Contemporary Reflection*.
12. Ibid., 24.
13. Ibid., 29–30. Here Perkins quotes Hans Kung, *On Being a Christian* (Garden City: Doubleday, 1976), 344–61.
14. Ibid., 84.

come down to us."[15] Perkins assumes a kind of transcendentalism in which the great resurrection themes of the transcendence of death, the triumph of good over evil, and the liberation of humanity are sufficient for faith without the credibility of the resurrection as a historical event.[16] Ultimately, Perkins insulates theological concerns from historical research by making history largely irrelevant to faith.

Pinchas Lapide claims that most objections to the historicity of the resurrection miss their target in that "they attempt to understand 'reality' in a restricted way, exclusively as a physically comprehensible or rationally understandable facticity—a standard which is hostile to all human faith."[17] This lack of empathy with the *historical* reality that all the witnesses to the resurrection were "sons and daughters of Israel" prevents the historian from appreciating the developing tradition of belief in the resurrection of the dead in Jewish circles, a belief grounded in the love and power of God, which enabled the first disciples to believe not merely that Jesus *happened* to be raised from the dead but that he *must* have been raised from the dead, because he was the Messiah. For Lapide, the historicity of the resurrection of Jesus is confirmed by the use of the criterion of embarrassment: if the resurrection narratives were fictitious inventions, they would not have women be the first to find the empty tomb, they would not have had Jesus appear only to his disciples, and they *would* have had people brought to faith immediately by seeing the empty tomb. Despite all the literary embellishments, in the oldest records there remains a recognizable historical kernel which cannot simply be demythologized. While Lapide excludes certain elements—the earthquake, the angelic appearances, the ascension—as later embellishment, he concludes that the hypothesis of a bodily resurrection of Jesus caused by divine agency is in fact the best historical hypothesis by which to explain the data.

As a an observant religious Jew, however, Lapide does not feel compelled to share the Christian *interpretation* of Jesus' resurrection. He conjectures that God raised up Jesus in order to give birth to Christianity, "to carry the message of Sinai into the world. . . . Jesus therefore, without doubt, belongs to the *praeparatio messianic* of the full salvation which is still in the future."[18] He accepts "neither the messiahship of Jesus for the people

---

15. Ibid., 94, 115.
16. Cf. Conway and Ryan, *Karl Rahner*, 42–43.
17. Lapide, *Resurrection of Jesus*, 42–43.
18. Ibid., 92.

of Israel nor the Pauline interpretation of the resurrection of Jesus."[19] My appraisal is that Lapide discounts the eschatological dimension of the assertion that what Jesus experienced was *resurrection* rather than revivification, in order to discount the messianic claims made by or about Jesus. In the end, by choosing to regard particularly problematic miraculous elements such as the rending of the temple veil, the earthquake, or the raising to life of the dead as recorded in Matthew's Gospel, as unhistorical and therefore without theologically informative value, Lapide insulates his own religious concerns from the historical claims of the Gospels.

While these New Testament scholars employ very different arguments, none are explicit about their historical method (though Lapide at least raises some important methodological issues). In some important respects, these authors leave unanswered questions raised by the First Quest. None of them identify what they would consider to be essential elements of a depiction of the historical Jesus. None of them positively outlines the relationship of theological concerns to historical research. None of them declares what the relationship of the historical Jesus ought to be to the church's faith.

CRITIQUING THEOLOGICAL CONCERNS WITH HISTORICAL RESEARCH

Some recent New Testament scholars seek to critique theological concerns with historical research. This need not imply that they are hostile to Christian faith, though it is far more common in the case of the resurrection of Jesus to find this kind of critique aimed at the orthodox understanding.

John Dominic Crossan's historical method involves attempting to reconstruct the earliest forms of Christian faith, allowing for the interplay of *macrocosmic* level of social anthropology, the *mesocosmic* level of Greco-Roman history, and the *microcosmic* level of selected literary sources. Crossan explicitly aligns himself with Strauss and Bultmann in his commitment to tracing the development of the Christian tradition in its stages, including

> one of recording at least the essential core of words and deeds, events, and happenings; another of development, applying such data to new situations, novel problems, and unforeseen circumstances; and a final one of creation, not only composing new

19. Ibid., 152–53.

sayings and new stories, but, above all, composing larger complexes that changed their contents by that very process.[20]

The early Christians handled their source material with "a creative freedom we would never have dared postulate were it not forced upon us by the evidence.... The Gospels are neither histories nor biographies, even within the ancient tolerance of those genres."[21] Therefore, for the purposes of historical reconstruction, Crossan begins with a small catalogue of "complexes" of structurally, thematically, and imaginatively similar material that he and others have established through source and form criticism as authentic sources of information about the historical Jesus. These complexes consist primarily in non-canonical sources (those reconstructed by scholars from canonical sources and those the early church chose not to authorize). Crossan then prioritizes these sources from earliest to latest, and from most corroborated to least. From the earliest, most frequently corroborated material, Crossan discerns two themes that would make Jesus' ministry both intelligible in his context and distinctive enough to be noteworthy: the selflessness of his healing ministry, and his egalitarian practice of table fellowship: "The intersection of magic and meal, miracle and table is pointed directly at the intersection of patronage and clientele, honor and shame, the very heart of Mediterranean society."[22]

Given his privileging of non-canonical sources and his assumption of a developmental framework in the production of canonical sources, it is understandable that he arrives at a highly non-traditional picture of the historical Jesus: "We are forced then, by the primary stratum itself, to bring together two disparate elements: healer and Cynic, magic and meal. The historical Jesus was, then, a *peasant Jewish Cynic*."[23] This largely Greco-Roman, non-apocalyptic Jesus was arrested and crucified for disturbing the peace in the temple in a moment of "egalitarian rage," and tales of his arrest, trial, and crucifixion are "industrious redactions set out to solve one simple problem. *Nobody knew what happened to Jesus' body.*"[24] Crossan critiques the traditional picture of Jesus as being in control of his own destiny, and the orthodox understanding of the resurrection:

20. Crossan, *Historical Jesus*, xxxi.
21. Ibid., xxx.
22. Ibid., 304.
23. Ibid., 421.
24. Ibid., 324.

> If those who accepted Jesus during his earthly life had not continued to follow, believe, and experience his continuing presence after the crucifixion, all would have been over. That *is* the resurrection, the continuing presence in a continuing community of the past Jesus in a radically new and transcendental mode of present and future existence.[25]

Though Crossan presents his historical method as interdisciplinary, the heart of his reconstruction is almost exclusively rooted in the microcosmic level of literary criticism, with attention to the mesocosmic and macrocosmic levels arriving only secondarily. In order to fill out his picture of the historical Jesus, Crossan leans heavily upon the Gospel of Thomas, which most scholars believe was written in the second, not the first century, and his own literary reconstruction of "The Cross Gospel," which is rejected by the vast majority of scholars.[26] Further, Crossan never entertains doubts about his assumption that the earliest documents present the earliest, most authentic traditions, ignoring the likely role of oral tradition. In my opinion, Crossan's portrait of Jesus is not a simple matter of deduction from established facts, but rather a deliberate grouping of elements gathered in support of an unnamed hypothesis.

Gerd Lüdemann argues for a "public" debate about the resurrection of Jesus, that is, one available to the historian who is not theologically committed. Disregarding the resurrection narratives in the Gospels as lacking eyewitness-level credibility, Lüdemann turns to Paul's accounts of Jesus' resurrection appearances in order to "present a hypothesis on the 'resurrection' of Jesus which causes the least offence and solves the most difficulties."[27] Like Crossan, but more methodologically explicit, Lüdemann begins by identifying credible, relevant texts, and then applying redaction criticism, tradition criticism, and historical criticism. He then considers what he has left, namely reports of visionary appearances, of which some are more reliable than others, and reconstructs the earliest Christian testimony regarding the resurrection of Jesus from these.

Lüdemann therefore reads the Gospel narratives as mythological representations of selected visionary appearances, and concludes by identifying the "earliest Christian belief in the resurrection that God had taken [Jesus] to himself or exalted him, . . . which was unexpected after Jesus' death on

---

25. Ibid., 404.
26. Powell, *Jesus as a Figure in History*, 46. Cf. Evans, *Fabricating Jesus*, 78–85.
27. Lüdemann, *Resurrection of Jesus*, 15.

the cross."²⁸ Lüdemann chalks up any resistance to his hypothesis to the inability or unwillingness to appreciate the mystical, visionary character of Paul's personal piety. By making the earliest surviving *literary* attestation to the resurrection of Jesus definitive for all reports of the resurrection, Lüdemann uses historical research to critique theological considerations by confining the historicity of the resurrection to experiences of a particular kind, rendering any historical investigation into the resurrection narratives in the Gospels irrelevant to faith.

Willi Marxsen takes a slightly different route to the same destination as Crossan and Lüdemann. Marxsen begins by declaring that while "the resurrection of a dead person is, according to our experience, impossible . . . it is nonetheless inadmissible to make our (inevitably limited) experience the yardstick for what once happened and for the way it happened."²⁹ Rather than attempting to identify the earliest substratum of material underlying the Gospels, Marxsen reads the collection of Gospels as a literary whole. In spite of their contradictions, "one can see that *all the evangelists want to show that the activity of Jesus goes on.*"³⁰ Using this generalization, Marxsen metaphorizes Jesus' postmortem existence, and concludes that the activity of proclaiming and healing on the part of Jesus' disciples is the total reality of Jesus' resurrection.

Marxsen says that the historian who declares for or against the historicity of the resurrection has "exceeded the bounds of his potentialities."³¹ If the activity of the community *is* the resurrection of Jesus, the verification of the resurrection is not a historical question but an ethical question that is beyond the historian's discipline. It might seem that Marxsen has successfully side-stepped the question of the historicity of the resurrection, by concluding that the Gospels never intended to ask their readers to understand the resurrection of Jesus as a singular historical event. He refrains from condemning the Gospel narratives as misrepresenting *historical* events by denying this to be within their intended scope. He has, however, declared against the *orthodox* understanding of the resurrection when he concludes that the accounts of the resurrection should be read as metaphor rather than as historical reporting. Marxsen uses historical research to critique theological concerns and to support his *theological* assertion that "God can

---

28. Ibid., 176.
29. Marxsen, *Resurrection of Jesus of Nazareth*, 21.
30. Ibid., 77.
31. Ibid., 119.

do anything.... And that is far more than the idea of the resurrection of the dead could ever express."[32]

Amy-Jill Levine takes the hermeneutics of Crossan, Lüdemann, and Marxsen one step further. Levine asks the more radical question of what relevance, if any, the texts of the New Testament have for historical research. Ancient texts do not always present their contents with the modern question of historicity in mind: it may be that "either the authors are presenting the way they presume things once were; or they are depicting [their] present social circumstances masked by a fictional setting; or they are prescribing, through an appeal to the legitimation provided by time and tradition, the way they think people ought to behave."[33] Famously, Levine remarks on the potential disconnect of our modern questions and the offerings of the New Testament when she declares that "bad history cannot lead to good theology."[34]

Levine doubts that very much can be gained in the area of determining historical authenticity by exploring issues of literary dependence among the Gospels or form-criticism (historical evaluation based literary form) of various episodes within the Gospels. Levine dismisses the attempts of Käsemann and others to determine what belongs to the historical Jesus, saying we don't know enough about either first-century Judaism or the early church to form a concrete image from which the real Jesus might have differed. Levine has a high regard for the literary and theological merits of the Gospels, but her skepticism around the usefulness of various forms of literary and historical criticism, combined with her Troeltschian exclusion of the miraculous, leaves Levine with nothing on which to build a historical hypothesis. Though Levine has no declared theological agenda, her rejection of the applicability of historical method to the New Testament accounts of the resurrection *effectively* critiques those theological concerns that rely on the value of the New Testament as evidence to support the orthodox understanding of the resurrection.

These New Testament scholars employ progressively more subtle arguments, and are more explicit about the historical method they do (or decline to) employ. In some important respects, most of these authors mirror the Second Quest in seeking out the "authentic" proclamation of the early church regarding the resurrection of Jesus, but none of them, in my

---

32. Ibid., 188.
33. Levine, *Women Like This*, xii–xiii.
34. Levine, *Misunderstood Jew*, 173.

opinion, satisfactorily answer the question of why the early church would have wanted to mythologize the resurrection of Jesus in a way that would put them increasingly at odds with both their Jewish roots and their Greco-Roman milieu, namely, in claiming that Jesus' resurrection was a bodily event. Crossan, Lüdemann, and Marxsen assert that this was never the actual intention of the earliest Christian sources, but rather a later development; Levine doubts that we'll ever know.

INTEGRATING THEOLOGICAL CONCERNS AND HISTORICAL RESEARCH

Some recent New Testament scholars seek to integrate theological concerns and historical research. This need not imply that they think their theological concerns are primary and their historical research is secondary, but only that they acknowledge that theology and history overlap at many points, including their understanding of the resurrection of Jesus.

Nicholas Thomas Wright identifies his agenda as attempting to answer the following questions: (1) How does Jesus fit into first-century Judaism? (2) What were Jesus' aims? (3) Why did Jesus die? (4) How and why did the early church begin? And (5) Why are the Gospels what they are? Wright adds a sixth question to his own list that is not historical in nature, but always lurking just beneath the surface, that connects the agenda of historical research with theological concerns: "How does the Jesus we discover by doing 'history' relate to the contemporary church and world?"[35] Wright lays out his historical method more clearly than most New Testament scholars, crediting his mentor Ben Meyer (who in turn credits his studies with Bernard Lonergan).[36] Wright says that historians can neither function as naïve realists, as if the historians own views are not actually in play, nor be trapped in a world of phenomenalism and structuralism, where there is no hope of historical reconstruction reflecting real history. Rather, historians must engage in self-aware critical reflection on their perception of the evidence, naming their biases for all to see, in examining or creating any hypothesis. A good hypothesis, expressed in narrative form, is the crowning work of the historian:

---

35. Wright, *Jesus and the Victory of God*, 117.
36. Meyer, *Aims of Jesus*. Cf. Meyer, *Critical Realism and the New Testament*.

The Employment of History

> There are three things a good hypothesis (in any field) must do.... First, it must include the data.... Second, it must construct a basically simple and coherent overall picture.... [Third,] the proposed explanatory story must prove itself fruitful in other related areas, must explain or help to explain other problems.[37]

There are many things in history that have no analogy, Wright says, and the historian may choose to be open to the idea that the resurrection is one of those.

Examining the evidence, Wright creates the hypothesis that the bodily resurrection of Jesus best explains how Christianity started and why it took the shape the way it did: it takes account of what first-century Jews understood by resurrection; it offers a comprehensible starting point for the theological development of the church; and it is supported by different forms and streams of evidence that are reasonably coherent but do not bear the marks of being contrived. Wright acknowledges that as a historian he works in probabilities, but that his hypothesis requires him to constrict the Troeltschian principle of analogy to a rule of thumb rather than an absolute principle, to allow for the effectiveness of divine action. Wright goes so far as to say that even without divine action, the bodily resurrection of Jesus would still be the best hypothesis to answer the question of why and how the church started. It is noteworthy that the historical questions Wright poses of the available data are the theological questions that the New Testament texts wrestle with: it is no surprise, then, that his hypothesis is aligned with the answers the texts provide. This alignment does not necessarily render Wright's hypothesis invalid; in fact, it may be more thoroughly inclusive of the *historical* concerns of the New Testament authors.

John P. Meier presents at the beginning of his magnum opus the image of "an unpapal enclave" comprised of a Protestant, a Catholic, a Jew, and an agnostic, to whom he would like to present a satisfactory picture of Jesus. He quickly qualifies that intention, however, recognizing that his attempt to stand apart from any faith-stance "is itself a 'faith stance' in the wide sense of the phrase.... There is no neutral Switzerland of the mind in the world of Jesus research."[38] Meier is aware that selection of data is already interpretation of data, that no historical figure can be reduced to the intersection of various social, cultural, and political conditions. He also acknowledges that the Gospels are not unvarnished chronicles: "to speak of the Gospel writers

---

37. Wright, *Resurrection of the Son of God*, 99–100.
38. Meier, *Marginal Jew*, 5.

as presenting or intending to present the historical Jesus transports them in an exegetical time machine to the Enlightenment."[39] He is skeptical of efforts to reconstruct a core of Jesus' sayings from literary criticism because they leave out the obvious presence of oral tradition. He is scornful of using later, apocryphal Gospels to search for the historical Jesus: "Critics like Crossan, Koester, and James M. Robinson are simply on the wrong track."[40] Meier does, however, make use of a number of tools of historical criticism, including the criteria of embarrassment, discontinuity, multiple attestation, coherence, traces of Aramaic, evidence of the Palestinian environment, vividness in narration, development of tradition and, most interestingly, service to the rationale for Jesus' rejection and execution—the central fact that each Gospel takes pains to explain.[41]

Unlike Wright, Meier formally excludes the resurrection narratives from historical consideration, saying, "The restrictive definition of the historical Jesus I will be using does not allow us to proceed into matters that can only be affirmed by faith."[42] Deeper into his work, however, he temporarily and self-consciously removes his "exegetical" hat and dons his "theological" hat in order to say:

> The "real" has been defined—and has to be defined—in terms of what exists within this world of time and space, what can be experienced in principle by any observer, and what can be reasonably deduced or inferred from such experience. Faith and Christian theology, however, affirm ultimate realities beyond what is merely empirical or provable by reason: e.g., the triune God and the risen Jesus.[43]

Thus while admitting that *some* kind of faith-stance is ingredient to all historical work, Meier strives to neutralize his own faith stance while he works as a historian, according to the normal limitations of that discipline. However, echoing Balthasar's comment about a historian's parameters being adequate to the subject matter, Meier points to his own personal conviction that a *complete* historical investigation of Jesus, which would include his purported predictions of his resurrection and claims to have risen, can

---

39. Ibid., 26.
40. Ibid., 122.
41. Ibid., 168–84.
42. Ibid., 13.
43. Ibid., 197.

only be done with an expansion of historical method that would include theological considerations.

Marcus J. Borg considers the Gospels to contain both (1) history, consisting in narratives that we, in our modern sense, might call historical narratives, and (2) history metaphorized, consisting in narratives in which a historical incident has been recast in mythical terms to help the reader grasp its significance. In this way, the Gospel narratives flesh-out the theological implications of the historical understanding of Jesus that we can otherwise derive from literary criticism of the Gospels. Borg's view of the historical Jesus is of a non-messianic, non-eschatological "spirit-person," calling people to "a non-material level of reality." Jesus was a "teacher of wisdom," calling people to a first-hand experience of God. Jesus was a "social prophet," arguing for an ethic of compassion to overtake an ethic of ritual purity. Jesus was a "movement founder," creating a radically inclusive community. In self-awareness, Borg asserts:

> The image of Jesus I have sketched in the preceding chapters is quite different from the popular understanding of Jesus, the Jesus many of us have met before. His own self-understanding did not include thinking and speaking about himself as the Son of God whose historical intention or purpose was to die for the sins of the world, and his message was not about believing in him.[44]

Borg distinguishes between the "pre-Easter Jesus" and the "post-Easter Jesus." The pre-Easter Jesus is the Jesus of history, the person that the disciples knew before his death and the Jesus that the public met. The post-Easter Jesus is the *experience* of Jesus as a spiritual reality. The Gospel narratives of the resurrection are spiritual experiences recast as narratives, which don't require the supposition that anything remarkable happened to Jesus' corpse. Borg wants to assert, more explicitly than Lüdemann and Marxsen, that the disciples truly encountered the person of Jesus, and not just their own memories of Jesus, or the truth about Jesus. Christian faith, according to Borg, is not a set of beliefs about Jesus, but the encounter with him that God has made available to us. Though Borg's understanding of the resurrection may not be completely orthodox, it does require theological concerns to be brought to historical research in order to understand the resurrection as Jesus' disciples experienced it—and as we can experience it.

Udo Schnelle maintains that there is no such thing as a historical investigation into the life and ministry of Jesus that is not at the same time

---

44. Borg, *Meeting Jesus Again for the First Time*, 117.

theological. Schnelle acknowledges that there is both history and theologically charged metaphor in the Gospels, but contends that these cannot be separated according to our modern sensibilities without destroying the Gospel's authorial integrity. Further, the move to identify authentic sayings of Jesus without simultaneously identifying authentic *actions* of Jesus is a mistake that leaves his sayings without a life-context in which to understand them. According to Schnelle, every historical hypothesis about Jesus "must explain the different perceptions of his life and ministry that Jesus triggered both before and after Easter, and must offer a plausible account of the differing ways in which his post-Easter interpreters related their interpretations of the pre-Easter Jesus."[45] For Schnelle, the resurrection is an ontologically separate event from the post-Easter appearances of Jesus, and the appearances were of such a quality that they invoked the language of resurrection.[46]

Although he stresses the ontological independence of the resurrection of Jesus from resurrection-faith, Schnelle acknowledges that facts do not interpret themselves. Schnelle explicitly sides with Pannenberg in denying that historical investigation into the resurrection of Jesus is somehow illegitimate—in which case, "the resurrection is left in the rubble of bygone history, and when the connection to an original event is severed, faith becomes merely an ideological assertion."[47] Recognizing the constructed nature of history, Schnelle insists that the only way to deal with the awkward facticity of the resurrection is to understand it as a "transcendent" event which, "although it cannot be subsumed [*einordnen*] under the categories of human reality, it can be coordinated [*zuordnen*] with them." By this Schnelle means the resurrection of Jesus must be understood as "the act of God who transcends his own eternity."[48] For Schnelle, theological concerns and historical research *must* accompany one another in the case of the resurrection for any kind of comprehensibility.

---

45. Schnelle, *Theology of the New Testament*, 68.
46. Ibid., 168.
47. Ibid., 236.
48. Ibid., 238.

The Employment of History

SOME HIGH-LEVEL OBSERVATIONS ABOUT THEOLOGICAL CONCERNS AND HISTORICAL RESEARCH

My gathering of these New Testament scholars into these categories is less than perfect, and may well have been affected by my prior understanding of the three "Quests" for the historical Jesus. However, there is another set of correlations that I would like to make, that cuts across the three categories of "insulating," "critiquing," and "integrating." These correlations will not necessarily simplify the overall picture, but they may explain why bells of recognition may have sounded here and there as you patiently ploughed through this chapter.

It seems to me that Craig and to a greater extent Habermas employ a *traditional* historical method. That is, they deal with the New Testament in a relatively uncritical way, amassing sources in a cumulative rather than a qualitative fashion, and their theological considerations are assumed rather than argued for. There is also a certain tone of "rightness" to their work, as if the reasons for holding to the orthodox understanding of the resurrection simply need to be supported, and all will be well. Lapide also keeps to orthodoxy, but it is understandably his own Jewish orthodoxy that prevails, though he has been more creative in reinterpreting his tradition than Craig or Habermas.

Crossan, Lüdemann, and Marxsen clearly employ modern historical method. They believe that whatever their own preconceptions, the facts can and do "speak for themselves" and compel them to their conclusions. Their historical research is conducted using the Troeltschian principles, which excludes the miraculous; they are largely precluded from entertaining the orthodox understanding of the resurrection and, since all three consider themselves to be Christians, arrive at a revisionist view of the resurrection.

Perkins and Levine, although they address the relationship of theological concerns and historical research quite differently, both wind up in a kind of postmodern detachment from historical reference. Perkins uses a structuralist approach that precludes her from addressing the question of historical facticity. Levine says that she would be happy to address the question of historical facticity, but says that the sources aren't suitable for that purpose.

Wright, Meier, Borg, and Schnelle are all working, in their own ways, in what I have labeled a Third Millennium historical method, willing to take

89

The Resurrection of History

into account their own perspective and recognize that there is more to historical reality than the modern approach can allow. Borg and Schnelle may be the happiest to admit working in this new method; Wright is cautiously accepting of the integration of history and theology in his work; Meier would prefer to have associate membership in the Third Millennium club.

In case you missed it along the way, or in case I haven't said it clearly enough, many historians and New Testament scholars will not be able to entertain the orthodox understanding of the resurrection of Jesus, simply because their methodological assumptions don't allow it. These writers include those who consider themselves Christians, who may or may not hold the orthodox understanding of the resurrection, but believe they are being faithful to the demands of their discipline. These scholars may need to come to grips with the resurrection of history before they can come to grips with the history of the resurrection.

QUESTIONS FOR CONSIDERATION

Seminary

1. What is your assessment of efforts to find "the historical Jesus" through literary and historical criticism?
2. What do you think are some of the elements of a sound historical method?

Study Group

1. In your mind, to what extent do the Gospels portray the historical Jesus?
2. If another Gospel was discovered, and it could be determined that it was written before Matthew, Mark, Luke, and John, would you favor it being put in the Bible?

Individual

1. In what ways does the idea that the historical Jesus might be different from the Jesus of the Gospels bother you?
2. How has your personal picture of Jesus changed over the course of your life?

6 The Enjoyment of History

THE PARISH HALL IS packed, with an audience of parents, grandparents, uncles and aunts, little brothers and sisters still too young to participate. Cameras are double-checked, and at the ready. The lights dim, and the curtain opens. On stage is a girl in an oversized peasant dress, with a light blue shawl. She is seated, with her sewing on her lap. She is looking dreamily off into the distance, when from stage right a boy enters wearing a white choir gown, and a tinsel-garland crown. Before a word is spoken, you know the young woman is Mary, and the young man is Gabriel. "Funny," you think to yourself, "I never pictured an angel wearing glasses. Or wearing sneakers." The actors speak a little too softly, and their lines are slightly garbled, and once or twice a scene they look offstage where a Sunday School teacher is motioning frantically. Everyone laughs a little when one of the shepherds turns to wave at his mother. But it doesn't matter. It is Christmas, and this is *the* story of the season, the same story you acted out when you were young, with your parents watching, a generation ago.

You barely notice anymore that the story combines elements that are within your experience, such as the anxiety of a father, the joy of a mother, the birth of a child, with elements that you can more easily picture, such as the paranoia of a ruler, along with elements almost beyond your imagination, such as the appearance of heavenly hosts. You have been shaped by this story: it lives inside you, and informs your worldview, even if you have never thought much about what "could have" or "must have" *really* happened. You may even shrug off such questions as if they don't matter. After all, the point is that Jesus was born. Other narrative elements, such as the virginity of Mary, the location of the birth in Bethlehem, and the murderous reaction of Herod all help define the significance of Jesus' birth, but few people dispute that Jesus was in fact born in a manner consistent with that of other human beings, and so lived, and so died.

The resurrection of Jesus, however, is a different matter. To use Aristotelian/scholastic language, the potential of Jesus rising from the dead in human form is not natural. We don't expect it to be predictable from, or explainable by, natural causes. The claim that Jesus was raised from the dead presumes the accessibility of the "natural" sphere by divine power. The historical claims of the New Testament appear to be that something "super-natural" occurred postmortem in the case of Jesus. Exactly what reality those historical claims name, imply, or indicate is the subject of much debate.

So far I have argued in chapter 2, "History Matters," that history is vitally important to how we live our lives as individuals and in society. In chapter 3, "The History of History," through our survey of dominant historians and historiographers, I have argued that there has been some notable evolution in what accepted historical method includes and excludes. In chapter 4, "The Theology of History," through our survey of dominant twentieth-century theologians, I have argued that theology is an essential ingredient in historical research, especially when it comes to historical claims that challenge reigning metaphysical assumptions. In chapter 5, "The Employment of History," through our survey of contemporary New Testament scholars, I have argued that the way in which theological concerns are included or excluded greatly affects the potential results of historical research, especially when it comes to the resurrection of Jesus. In this chapter I conduct a brief survey of contemporary theologians on the subject of the historicity of the resurrection of Jesus. I begin with an article by Allan Padgett that I think sets up the major issues, and then proceed through a series of scholarly consideration before arriving at my destination which, if you hadn't discerned it already, is that, with appropriate qualification and self-identification, the resurrection of Jesus can be considered as a historical event by means of historical research.

ALAN G. PADGETT: ADVICE FOR RELIGIOUS HISTORIANS

In "Advice for Religious Historians: On the Myth of a Purely Historical Jesus," Padgett begins by asking his fellow theologians to acknowledge the passing of modernity:

The Resurrection of History

> At one time in our Western universities we were certain of how history should proceed, as a rigorous, value-free, scientific discipline. But that era is now over. How shall we proceed? Does "anything go" in historical research now that modernity is over? How shall we understand the discipline of religious *history* in a post-positivist, post-modern situation? For modernity, with its faith in reason and its myth of neutral, scientific scholarship, is well and truly dead. *Requiescat in pace*.[1]

He then proposes to use the resurrection of Jesus as his test-case for "examining the myth of a purely historical approach to religious studies." In analyzing this "myth," Padgett lists three assumptions that underlay that myth:

> (1) That religious faith distorts scientific, critical scholarship; (2) because this is true, the only proper, academic, scientific methodology in religious studies is one that rejects religious faith itself; (3) that a purely historical, scientific, faith-free and value-neutral methodology is available to us in what we might broadly call the social-scientific disciplines.[2]

Padgett raises the example of former president Richard Nixon to illustrate how there is really no neutrality in any historical research. Few American researchers would have no prior impressions of Nixon's time in office, and even a relatively naïve researcher would have difficulty in finding any genuinely unbiased sources. In the case of historical research into the life of Jesus, "important advances have been made," but the "El Dorado" of neutrality remains elusive. Padgett criticizes those on the right (e.g., Habermas) and the left (e.g., Marxsen) for engaging in what he calls "the neutrality two-step," wherein, "having recognized the prejudice of perspective, . . . scholars still seem to hope that our biases and prejudices can be overcome through careful religious neutrality and scientific method."[3] Padgett wonders aloud as to why this imaginary neutrality is even thought to be desirable, ignoring the obvious possibility that Christian faith might actually give us *better* insight into the historical Jesus.

Padgett expresses his displeasure with what he characterizes as Meier's attempt to "dance around" the prejudice of perspective by appealing to a "consensus Jesus," namely, the historical Jesus known to us by a consensus of

---

1. Padgett, "Advice for Religious Historians," 288.
2. Ibid., 290.
3. Ibid., 293.

New Testament scholarship: "As any first-year philosophy student knows," says Padgett disdainfully, "the consensus theory of truth is bogus. . . . At the practical end, we always have to ask the critical . . . question: who defines the consensus?"[4] Padgett also disparages the relentless, mechanical application of the hermeneutic of suspicion: it is one thing to be *critical* of historical sources, but it is another to consistently take a "guilty until proven innocent" approach to the New Testament. In the search for the historical Jesus, this is poisoning the well, rendering our best sources of historical data useless for historical research. We could proceed as if by eliminating all religious faith—our own or that embedded in the sources—we would in the end somehow have a "scientific" understanding of the historical Jesus, but we would, if we were successful, in all likelihood wind up with a product that no one should want, a mere blank screen accommodating the projection of our own contemporary values. This is not something we should strive for. Western scholarship, says Padgett, needs to *name* and *reclaim* the values it wants to employ in its efforts. "Science and technology, divorced from religious wisdom and moral values, constitute not only a myth, but the nightmare of the twentieth century."[5]

Padgett understands how connected the debate over the relationship of history and religious faith is to the debate over the relationship of science and religious faith. Scientists no less than historians must admit the "prejudice of perspective," and acknowledge that even science is done through a plurality of worldviews. This may signal the end of some important methodological dimensions of the Enlightenment, but it is, according to Padgett, no cause for alarm: "Pluralism and prejudice of perspective should lead us to humility, but not despair or to relativism. Cognitive relativism does not follow from plurality or from the prejudice of perspective."[6] Knowing that the results of historical research are less certain because they are not entirely neutral doesn't mean that we are therefore not dealing with the real world, whether we work in modes of Christian, Marxist, or scientific materialist faith. As Padgett says, "I affirm objective truth; it is objective knowledge I object to." In the case of the resurrection of Jesus, Padgett says that

> if it did happen, it is not subject to natural-scientific explanation. Likewise, it is not subject to historical explanation. Historical science is incapable of making a theological judgement about

4. Ibid., 297.
5. Ibid., 299.
6. Ibid., 301.

> whether or not God could or did raise Jesus. . . . So we can and should accept the difference between natural-scientific, social scientific (including historical), and theological explanations.[7]

Padgett says in this vein that attempts to explain the resurrection historically without recourse to theology can lead to particularly tortured reconstructions. As an example, Padgett calls Lüdemann's understanding of the resurrection "far less likely than any miracle!"[8]

Finally, Padgett turns to the notion of religious faith. If "having faith" means having existential certainty, then, quite rightly, "faith cannot be based upon the probability arguments of history, philosophy, and science." In fact, Padgett even calls any demand for faith to provide existential certainty a grave mistake, one which divorces faith from rationality. Padgett says that although he would be willing to die for his faith, still his faith "must be open to rational reflection and revision in the light of reason, evidence, and argument . . . in more critical and reflective moments."[9]

Padgett represents what I have called Third Millennium historical method: he rejects the intellectual firewall between theological considerations and historical research. He celebrates "the prejudice of perspective," especially when it challenges the established consensus, and he affirms our ability to be in touch with the world around us. On this last point, Padgett credits Ben Meyer as having more than anyone else introduced the epistemology of critical realism to the Western academy: "Ben Meyer points us to the proper way out of this fear in his review of criteria of indices of authenticity: not to shun subjectivity, but to embrace it as a moment on the way toward objectivity."[10] The function of tradition, Padgett says, is to take up our individual perspectives into a larger discourse to be encountered by more comprehensive understandings of the truth, so that we may correct and be corrected by the understandings and misunderstandings of others. If we were to map Padgett's understanding of historical research onto McIntires's historical method, we would find that in Padgett's terminology natural sciences frame the *ontological* dimension of an event, social sciences frame the *temporal* dimension of an event, and philosophical and theological sciences frame the *ultimate* dimension of an event.

---

7. Ibid., 303–4.
8. Ibid., 305.
9. Ibid., 305–6.
10. Ibid., 300.

THE RESURRECTION AS CONTINUING PRESENCE

The issues identified by Padgett are dealt with differently by various contemporary theologians.

Peter Carnley offers a strong and thorough attempt to come to grips with the historicity of the resurrection of Jesus. He states the need for historical research to penetrate behind the Gospels' various redactional (editorial) viewpoints to the original experience of the resurrection. He also affirms that historical criticism alone is inadequate for a complete analysis of the Easter event, and that the element of religious faith must come into view. In Carnley's mind, three potential approaches to the resurrection of Jesus fall short in one way or another. First, the category of history taken by itself is insufficient to describe the resurrection, since the focus of history is the singular event, and the resurrection is comprised of not merely the empty tomb but the repeated revelatory appearances of the post-Easter Jesus. Second, the category of eschatology taken by itself is insufficient, since the resurrection appearances, while eschatological in character, are referred to as having occurred in time and space, with temporal effects. Third, declaring the resurrection to be a non-event is insufficient since all the evidence that we have describes the resurrection as having both objective and subjective dimensions.

Carnley concurs with Edward Schillebeeckx that the resurrection is portrayed in the New Testament as essentially a communal experience among the believing disciples. He disagrees, however, with Marxsen's reductionistic approach, in which "the faith-response of Christians must be resolved into a single pattern constituted by the central idea of the 'hearing of the proclamation,' and cannot be an assent based on evidence. This leads to the effective neutralization of the appearances tradition, which remains as a persistent and embarrassing datum in the primitive accounts of faith."[11] While Carnley notes the variations in the responses of the disciples, he opposes the idea that the appearances were therefore objectively different: "I do not think it is satisfactory either historically or dogmatically to accept the suggestion that qualitatively quite different experiences were given to different people, so that some might be said to have encountered Jesus in a concrete, material form and others in a more ethereal, visionary, or spiritual form." Carnley prefers to speak of "a variety of attempts to visualize and

---

11. Carnley, *Structure of Resurrection*, 167.

articulate what was essentially 'heavenly' and ambiguous and thus open to a range of speculative interpretations and developments."[12]

For Carnley, while there may be historical particularity (eventfulness) to the disciples' *experiences*, historical particularity should not be objectified into the appearances of Jesus. Carnley has an explicitly theological motive for this suggestion, namely, to identify our present experience of the historical Jesus with the historical Jesus, and to integrate our remembrance of the historical Jesus into our present experience of him. In this way, "Easter faith" is the active remembering of Jesus in the life of the church and the reception of the self-giving Jesus through preaching and sacramental participation. For Carnley, the reality of the resurrection is both past *and* present, while it points to the future:

> The failure of the attempt to "prove" the occurrence of the resurrection by employing the historical model exclusively . . . has the positive effect of preventing us from "naturalizing" the resurrection, which, as we have seen, is an inexorable gravitational pull of any attempt to handle the mystery of the resurrection by this means alone. Such an approach must be complemented by alternative avenues of approach, that are not only more appropriate to its nature as an eschatological event, but also appropriate to the apprehension of a present reality and not just to the handling of an occurrence in the past. This means that we must incorporate epistemology into our understanding of faith, as well as attempting to approach it in a purely retrospective, historical-theological way.[13]

In this proposal, Carnley wants to preserve the dimension of God's activity in the disciples' experience of the resurrection alongside God's activity in making Jesus genuinely present to the church in every generation.

What Carnley wants to avoid is declaring the resurrection to be a completely *public* event, completely accessible without theology through means of historical research, because this would allow anyone and everyone to claim their understanding of the resurrection to be equally authoritative as that of the Christian community. If that were the case, the historical Jesus would not be authentically remembered as the one who came to create that new community. The *message* of community must be embodied in the *medium* of community. For Carnley, the presence of Jesus, in his appearances to his disciples in the first hours and days following the crucifixion

---

12. Ibid., 241.
13. Ibid., 365.

and throughout the centuries, taken as a whole, *is* the resurrection. Peter Schmidt and Xavier Leon Dufour develop positions similar to that of Carnley's. Schmidt places the resurrection of Jesus in the same category as Jesus' presence in the Eucharist, being "real" without being empirical: in the resurrection, "we are dealing with an objective reality, but this reality as such is not understandable outside of faith."[14] Dufour makes the subtle move of reminding us that, in historical terms, a body is constituted by the various relationships it establishes: "Through both kerygma and Eucharist it is the same Jesus of Nazareth, who God raised from the dead and who, in the form of the Word and in the form of the act, makes himself present here and now."[15]

The understanding of the resurrection forwarded by Carnley, Schmidt, and Dufour has many attractive elements. It seeks to unify past and present experience of Jesus, dissolve the tension between "the Jesus of history" and "the Christ of faith," and incorporate the theological concerns of ecclesiology and community. The connection of Jesus' resurrection-life with his sacramental Presence is also welcome. It does, however, threaten to obliterate the *historicity* of the resurrection; if the true object of history is the singular event, and the singularity of the resurrection is swallowed up by its theological significance, the temporal, and perhaps the ontological, uniqueness of the resurrection event is lost or in high need of redefinition. If the resurrection event is redefined in a way that effectively cuts it off from historical research, it is no longer subject to critique from outside the community of faith, and runs the risk of becoming an unhistorical ideological symbol.

Gerald O'Collins stakes out yet another position. He takes on historians who would seek to discount the eventfulness of the resurrection by translating it into merely psychological events on the one hand or into first-century mythological developments on the other. At the same time, however, he takes on those who would seek to prove the facticity of the resurrection purely through historical research:

> The resurrection is not an event *in* space and time and hence should not be called "historical" [because] through the resurrection Christ passes out of the empirical sphere of this world to a new mode of existence in the "other" world of God. He moves outside the world and its history, outside the ordinary, datable,

14. Schmidt, "Interpretation of the Resurrection," 78.
15. Dufour, *Resurrection and the Message of Easter*, 244.

localizable conditions of our experience—to become an "otherworldly" reality.[16]

O'Collins argues that God's movements in the lives of historical figures such as Abraham, Moses, and Isaiah do not make God's existence historical. Similarly, the appearances of Jesus to his disciples "are not historical from his side, even if they do form part of the history of Peter, Paul, and the other witness of the risen Lord."[17]

O'Collins does argue for the historicity of the empty tomb, and of the experience of those who saw the resurrected Jesus. From this it could be inferred that O'Collins would allow a historian to frame a hypothesis around the experience of the witnesses. Elsewhere O'Collins upholds the record of the women as the first witnesses of the resurrection, even accusing those who would discount their testimony as sexist.[18] He might appreciate David Fergusson's comment on their testimony, who notes that the employment of the empty tomb as a symbol does not entail that it was "originally devised by the community for that purpose.... It could even be that there is a valid argument running in the opposite direction, viz., that in order to function adequately as vehicles of proclamation these narratives must be modelled on some historical reminiscence."[19]

O'Collins seems to be arguing for an understanding of the resurrection of that is not a historical event but somehow is presented by or testified to by historical events. If what O'Collins means to do is deny that the historian *as historian*, that is, through historical research alone, has no right to infer divine causality, he is standing on the same ground as Meier, Tilley, and many others who are not willing to embrace the Third Millennium historical method. And if he means to assert that the ongoing, post-resurrection life of Jesus is not accessible through historical research unless theological considerations are declared and brought into play, I would deem him to be on safe ground. However, if he means to place the *event* of Jesus' resurrection outside "space and time," he risks sacrificing the objectivity of the resurrection and effectively insulates all theological concerns from the impact of historical research, leaving the same unanswered questions as Carnley, Schmidt, and Dufour. While I sympathize with the motives of O'Collins, his theological approach does not, in my opinion, allow for the distinct

---

16. O'Collins, "Is the Resurrection an 'Historical Event'?," 319.
17. Ibid., 320.
18. O'Collins, "Resurrection: The State of the Questions," 7.
19. Fergusson, "Interpreting the Resurrection," 302.

The Enjoyment of History

historical eventfulness of the resurrection of Jesus that the New Testament presents as ingredient to the earliest Christian proclamation.

THE RESURRECTION ACCOUNTS AS TESTIMONY

Peter F. Craffert looks at the vehicle of testimony from the perspective of cultural competence, saying that the only legitimate way to receive the New Testament testimonies concerning the resurrection of Jesus is as authentic to the culture of the witnesses. An anthropologist, says Craffert, on receiving testimony as to unusual occurrences, can (1) refer to them as real, which would be inauthentic for the anthropologist but affirming of the authenticity of those reporting; (2) refer to them as wrong or mythical, which would be authentic for the anthropologist but denigrating of those reporting, or (3) recognize that these occurrences are real and constitutive of reality *for those reporting them*, in the same sense as the anthropologist's beliefs are real and constitutive of the his or her reality.

According to Craffert, understanding this "cultural-sensitive" approach allows us to observe several things about the New Testament testimonies. With regard to the empty tomb, we can say, "If Jesus had appeared to so many people and after death continued a bodily existence as reported by the visions, it was obvious for them that the tomb must have been empty. They lived by a different logic."[20] That is, given the interest in bodily resurrection, visionary appearances of Jesus would have been enough for the first Christians to conclude and authentically testify that Jesus had risen bodily from the dead. Craffert goes on to decry the "ethnocentric disbelief" of critical New Testament scholarship, as well as the "ethnocentric belief" of orthodox New Testament scholarship, upholding as an alternative the "polyphasic" appreciation of the authentic cultural relativity inherent in the "social-scientific perspective" that allows for visionary appearances of Jesus naturally implying his bodily resurrection.

While Craffert's approach does commendably remind the historical researcher and the theologian to mind the gap between the present-day Western academy and first-century Judaism, his argument includes several unsubstantiated claims. First, it assumes a certain functionality of resurrection-belief within first-century Judaism wherein postmortem appearances would be interpreted as bodily resurrection, something not contemplated, so far as we know, in the interpretation of the narratives of Samuel's

20. Craffert, "Did Jesus Rise Bodily from the Dead?," 140.

The Resurrection of History

appearance to Saul at Endor (1 Sam 28:3–25) and the raising of the widow's son by Elijah (1 Kgs 17:17–24). Second, it assumes a strange willingness on the part of first-century Jewish and Gentile hearers to believe without verification an astounding claim that was, in principle, at least partially falsifiable by locating Jesus' tomb. Third, it assumes a thorough disassociation in the practice of history writing on the part of the Gospel writers from Greco-Roman biography. Fourth, it assumes a radical distance between first-century Judaism and our present day in terms of the connection of evidence and historical inference. Finally, Craffert's approach assumes that New Testament scholarship should remain firmly within the naturalistic framework of the "social-scientific perspective" without reference to the relevance of theology.

Francis Schüssler Fiorenza considers the principal options of the relationship of historical research to theological considerations and proposes a substantially different approach from that of Carnley or O'Collins.[21] First, he describes how "Traditional Fundamental Theology" in the Roman Catholic tradition understands the resurrection to be the *ground* of faith: because we know by means *other than faith* (i.e., historical research) that Jesus rose from the dead, we can therefore generate faith in the risen Lord. This approach is easily undermined, however, by literary and historical criticism of the Gospels and puts the Christian faith at the mercy of the historians. Padgett might be comfortable on this footing, but Schüssler Fiorenza is not. Second, he describes how "Transcendental Fundamental Theology" understands the resurrection as an *object of faith* in its intrinsic revelatory significance, accessible to all as the affirmation of the human longing for permanence in the face of death: because we know by means *other than faith* that we need to have faith, we choose to take hold of faith in the risen Lord. This approach is soon undermined by the acknowledgement of a plurality of worldviews and their particular statements of existential questions and puts the Christian faith at the mercy of contemporary culture. Third, he describes how the "Contemporary Historical-Critical Approach" understands the resurrection as the result of reflection by the disciples on the identity of Jesus: *prior to having faith* we discover the demythologized message of the Christian faith, and we commit ourselves to this message *symbolically expressed as faith* in the risen Lord. This approach is immediately undermined by the historical claims of the Gospel accounts of an event far transcending a psychological occurrence.

---

21. Schüssler Fiorenza, *Foundational Theology and the Church*, 5–55.

The Enjoyment of History

To move past these options, Schüssler Fiorenza introduces the category of *testimony*. While historical investigation seeks to maximize accuracy and intelligibility by neutralizing the effects of the historian's interpretation, testimony unabashedly reports and interprets in the same action. In the New Testament we find testimonies concerning the resurrection of Jesus embodied in short doxological formulae that emphasize Jesus' eschatological significance, and narratives that emphasize continuity between Jesus and the church:

> The combination of the motifs of commissioning and identity show that the basic goal of the appearance stories is not to prove the resurrection of Jesus but to show the link between the Church's mission and the historical Jesus. The identity of the Risen Lord with the historical Jesus is the key to the appearance stories. . . . Faith in the resurrection has its ground within these testimonies rather than outside them.[22]

Employing the category of testimony is not the means of disenfranchising historical investigation; historical investigation may choose to discount the Christological dimensions of the resurrection accounts, but historical investigation can certainly bring the historian to the threshold of those theological considerations and present the historian with such historical questions as how and why the earliest church developed such a high Christology so early.[23]

Schüssler Fiorenza goes on to argue that believing the testimonies of the New Testament is to give primacy to the event of the resurrection, that is, to say that the resurrection gave rise to reflection on the life of Jesus, and not the other way around. These testimonies do not simply relate a past event within history, but report that an event has occurred that has fundamentally changed history itself. Affirming the resurrection of Jesus is to affirm that life is meaningful, and that "goodness and justice as the final ground of reality triumph over evil and injustice."[24] Encountering the risen Jesus caused the early Christians to comb back through the events in Jesus' life, to identify actions and words that confirmed this reality-changing event. The power of these testimonies, and not any "uninterpreted" or "real, historical" Jesus, says Schüssler Fiorenza, forms the ground of Christian faith.

---

22. Ibid., 38.
23. Schüssler Fiorenza, "Resurrection of Jesus and Roman Catholic Theology," 227.
24. Ibid., 43.

The Resurrection of History

Richard Bauckham agrees that in the case of the Gospels, "the kind of historiography they are is testimony."[25] Testimony doesn't present itself as disinterested and tentative, but asks in its very delivery to be trusted. In the case of the resurrection the testimony is asking the hearer to trust that the theological considerations are as pertinent as the historical details because they are not, in the mind of the witness, separable. Not all testimony is to be trusted, of course, and the evaluation of the trustworthiness of testimony involves corroboration, the credibility of the witness, the reasonableness of what is being testified to, and even the credibility of the community that credits the testimony. Schüssler Fiorenza expresses awareness that whether or not the testimonies of the New Testament are in fact trusted by historians is to some extent a matter of the historical method they employ, and what they would take to be a sufficient degree of certainty.

As a whole, Craffert's approach seems hopelessly mired in a kind of postmodern absolute perspectivalism, which discounts the ability of historical research to ever get at the truth about anything. Schüssler Fiorenza's understanding of testimony, on the other hand, takes account of the theologically concerned nature of the New Testament accounts of the resurrection of Jesus while maintaining the approachability of their historical referent by historical research.

THE RESURRECTION ACCOUNTS AS NARRATIVE

Hans Frei incorporates the category of testimony in developing his own approach to the question of the historicity of the Gospel accounts of the resurrection of Jesus. Frei sees a divide between conservative apologists who work to demonstrate (or assert theologically) that the true reference of scripture is to the objective facts of history, while liberal apologists strive to demonstrate (or assert theologically) that the true reference of Scripture is to theological or existential principles. Both are abusive of the very nature of the text, says Frei. In his literary reading of the Gospels, Frei argues that the Gospels present Jesus in a way that is not historical in the sense of being neutral about their subject, because Jesus is consistently portrayed as "the Risen One"; nor, however, do they present Jesus in mythological terms, without concern for historical referent. Rather, the Gospels are "history-like" because in the Gospel narratives "it is simply the unsubstitutable

---

25. Bauckham, *Jesus and the Eyewitnesses*, 5. Similar arguments could be made, presumably, for narrative elements related in the epistolary literature of the New Testament.

person about whom the story is told—his unsubstitutable deeds, words, and sufferings—that makes the real difference.[26]

> I believe one may affirm (a) that in the narrative the person of Jesus is available to us descriptively; (b) that there is identity between Jesus so described and the saviour's description; and hence, (c) there is continuity between Jesus and the proclamation of his name in the early community. I believe further that this descriptive availability, identity, and continuity represent not a transformation of Jesus into a myth but the demythologization of the saviour myth in the person of Jesus.[27]

Frei argues that rather than infer the true identity of Jesus from his words, we can and should take the more natural route of inferring the true identity of Jesus from the unity of his intentions and actions. According to Frei, the Gospels portray Jesus' identity as self-manifested in "(1) Jesus' obedience, (2) the coexistence of power and powerlessness, (3) the transition from one to the other, and (4) the interrelation of Jesus' and God's intention and action."[28] The real Jesus is not merely what he thought and taught, but how he acted and lived. The access to the identity of Jesus that the Gospels provide is not in the form that modern historical research would prefer, because modern historical criticism assumes that the real subject of inquiry is somehow "behind" the text, and needs to be uncovered. Frei calls this "subject-alienation," because the true subject is *other than* the depiction. Alternatively, in the literary criticism of a novel, the presumption is that the subject can be *identified* with the depiction. Frei calls this "subject manifestation," because the subject is as he or she is depicted.

According to Frei, the Gospels were written in the belief that the identity of Jesus was manifested in—and not obscured by—the details of his movements and action. In fact, Jesus is characterized as *unsubstitutable*: none other than this Jesus was (for God's purposes) the Crucified One, and he is now the Risen One. The Gospels are historical narratives, but they are not written according to the principle of authorial detachment which is emblematic of modern historical narrative. Michael Higton interprets Frei as contending that the Gospels present "a world in which there are not idealist reservations of the spirit cut off from the ceaseless ebb and flow of contingent events," which puts them at odds with the worldview

26. Ibid., 111.
27. Frei, *Identity of Jesus Christ*, 32.
28. Ibid., 164.

of post-Enlightenment developments in historical method. For Frei, "A Jesus who has not been raised is not *this* Jesus."²⁹ There is an absolutely critical historical claim bound up in Gospel accounts of the resurrection: to fail to read the implications of Jesus' resurrection back into the Gospels' testimony regarding Jesus is an inauthentic reading that results in the *total* disregard of the evangelists' depiction of Jesus.

Commenting specifically on the resurrection and its interpreters, Frei catalogues four views on the Gospels' depiction of the event: (1) *mythological*, referring to the "re-presentation" of Jesus as anywhere the life of faith is truly proclaimed and accepted; (2) *literal*, in which the subject matter of the texts and the reality they refer to are to be taken equally literally; (3) broadly *spiritual*, wherein "the reality is more important than the text and to be reconstructed through strict historical research together with philosophical speculation"; and (4) referring to a *real event*, "one to which human depiction and conceptions are inadequate, even though the literal one is the best that can be offered." Frei refers to this last option as "the adequate testimony to, rather than an accurate report of, the reality."³⁰ As testimony, the Gospel accounts of the resurrection of Jesus form a *necessary* but *not sufficient* condition for Christian faith—that is, they invite a positive faith-response, but don't by themselves force a faith-response.

Frei goes on to say that the New Testament accounts do not try to solve "the quandary of a live physical presence after death," but they "bear witness to the fact that Jesus, raised from the dead, was the same person, the same identity as before."³¹ In the end, however, Frei sounds a cautionary note regarding over-explaining the resurrection in historical terms: "It is well to understand this powerful assertion religiously rather than metaphysically, for metaphysical schemes, like myths, change but the Word of God abides."³² The testimony of the Gospels is not *how* God raised Jesus but *that* God raised Jesus. Higton probably captures the essence of Frei's position with regard to the resurrection narratives when he says that "by proclaiming a miracle in the midst of history, history is freed of the intolerable burden of somehow being *naturally* the home of the absolute, and so is allowed to be itself again."³³ By definitively breaking into history in the res-

---

29. Higton, *Christ, Providence, and History*, 110.
30. Frei, "How It All Began," 141.
31. Frei, *Identity*, 43.
32. Frei, "How It All Began," 144–45.
33. Higton, *Christ, Providence, and History*, 117.

urrection of Jesus, *God* has declared that the world is not a closed, perfect system, whose past can be perfectly discovered by the perfect application of a perfect historical method; historians will have to be content with doing their best in a world whose history can never be captured in any iron-clad, all-encompassing system of historical thought.

THE RESURRECTION AS A BODILY EVENT

One of the most stubborn dimensions of the Gospels' collective testimony to the resurrection of Jesus is that it is unabashedly depicted as a *bodily resurrection*. N. T. Wright wrestles with this dimension perhaps more than most interpreters, doing so from the critical-realist epistemology inherited from New Testament scholar Ben Meyer, who applied Lonerganian methodology to reading texts in the attempt to avoid postmodern skepticism on the one hand and naïve empiricism on the other:

> The object of interpretation has been a much-confused as well as much-disputed issue. We define it as *the intended sense of the text*. . . . When we speak of "the intended sense" (the object of the task of interpretation), we understand it to include tone, nuance, affirmation—in other words, the whole of textually realized intention. What must not be overlooked is that *affirmation—and so truth claim—is integral to the intended sense* of all texts to be interpreted, be they contemporary or no.[34]

In simplest terms, in reading New Testament texts, an interpreter's first responsibility is to determine as precisely as possible what the author has in fact managed to say, and then ask why it was said. In dialogue with Marcus Borg, Wright emphasizes that in order to do this properly the interpreter should first strive to appreciate the text in "emic" categories—that is, those native to the writer—rather than in the "etic" categories of the interpreter.[35] In the case of the resurrection, then, we must first sort out what the New Testament authors would most likely have understood by the very idea of resurrection.

Surveying Old Testament sources, Wright concludes that Israel's understanding of resurrection was *never* a disembodied afterlife. The hope for restoration of the nation's fortunes was perhaps the earliest understanding

---

34. Meyer, *Reality and Illusion*, 94, 96.
35. Borg and Wright, *Meaning of Jesus*, 226.

The Resurrection of History

of resurrection, but this soon generated the hope for the personal resurrection of those individuals who served God in exemplary fashion: "YHWH's answer to his people's exile would be, metaphorically, life from the dead (Isa 26, Ezek 37); YHWH's answer to people's martyrdom would be, literally, life from the dead (Dan 12)."[36] Examining sources from Second Temple Judaism (that is, later than 530 BCE), Wright points to various ideas of life after death, but when it comes to the use of the term "resurrection," he only finds plenty of confirmation, and no explicit contradiction, of the hope for individual immortality in terms of bodily resurrection from the grave "on the Last Day." Hebrew scholar J. L. Crenshaw concurs with Wright's analysis, saying that

> the powerful sense of communion with Yahweh and belief in the Deity's creative might and justice provided for the idea of an immortal soul and resurrection of the body. The catalyst that broke these ideas open and produced full-blown concepts of immortality and resurrection was apocalyptic theology, and its accompanying persecution of the righteous.[37]

Paul's correspondence, the earliest extant textual testimony to the resurrection of Jesus, shows clearly that Paul taught "a firm and sharply delineated belief in a past event, the resurrection of Jesus of Nazareth."[38] Wright belabors this point because so much exegetical work by others has proceeded on the assumption that the eventfulness, the historicity, of the resurrection can be ascribed to the creativity of the Gospel writers as they "mythologized" in narrative form the visionary experiences of the post-Easter Jesus. Rather, says Wright, the Gospels' emphases parallel those of Paul in both stressing the double meaning of resurrection carried over from the Old Testament and in adding the eventfulness of Jesus' resurrection.[39]

According to Paul and to the Gospels, what happened to Jesus, says Wright, was the resurrection of his body, in anticipation of the bodily resurrection forecast for all of God's people on the Last Day. Jews living in the time of Second Temple Judaism would have been exposed to various understandings of postmortem existence, including Platonic notes of freedom from bodily existence, the Sadducean understanding of immortality consisting in the continuation of one's family line or at least the memory

---

36. Wright, *Resurrection of the Son of God*, 127.
37. Crenshaw, "Love Is Stronger than Death," 71–72.
38. Wright, *Resurrection of the Son of God*, 374.
39. Ibid., 374.

of one's name, and various popular notions of ghosts. The understanding of "resurrection" allowed for some variation as well. Some held that the hope of resurrection was *confined* to the restoration of the nation's fortunes, citing Ezekiel 37; some held that only the righteous would experience resurrection, citing Psalm 37; some held that there would be a general resurrection, with a judgment of the righteous and the wicked, citing Psalm 1; some held that the souls of the righteous are held in heaven, awaiting reunion with their bodies laid in the earth, citing Psalm 50. Given the various options, both canonical and non-canonical first-century Christian sources present a remarkably unified understanding of Jesus' resurrection as a singular, bodily event—which is all the more surprising given that the *timing* of Jesus' resurrection did not precisely fit with any of those understandings otherwise present in first-century Judaism. This understanding of Jesus' resurrection, minus the attribution of metaphysical properties that would take place as much as a millennium later, was the "orthodox" understanding defended continuously from the early church fathers onward.

Wright does not minimize the challenge of trying to promote the idea of Jesus' bodily resurrection in the twenty-first century, to New Testament scholars, theologians, or anyone else: "To say, as the early Christians did, that the tomb was empty, and the 'meetings' with Jesus took place, because he had indeed been bodily raised from the dead, seems to require the suspension of all our normal language about how we know things about the past."[40] At times Wright employs the word "transformed" and even the neologism "transphysical" to allow *resurrection* to mean more in the case of Jesus than *resuscitation*. This need for a loose grip on the metaphysical reins, according to Wright, strengthens the historical hypothesis that Jesus was in fact raised from the dead: the early church was not making in the first instance a metaphysical claim (e.g., all people rise from the dead), but rather a singular claim about one person. The clumsy nature of the narratives themselves, and the obvious lack of effort on the part of the early church to homogenize them, grants them authenticity, inasmuch as they "have the puzzled air of someone saying, 'I didn't understand it at the time, and I'm not sure I do now, but this is more or less how it was.'"[41] Despite the temptation to weigh in dogmatically, Wright strives to stick to his stated task of constructing the best *historical* hypothesis to account for the particular testimonies of the first-century Christians that Jesus had been raised

---

40. Ibid., 710.
41. Ibid., 611.

from the dead. Knowing that there is no such thing as absolutely unconditioned historical research, Wright admits,

> I do not claim that [my reconstruction] constitutes a "proof" of the resurrection in terms of some neutral standpoint. It is, rather, a challenge to other explanations, other worldviews. . . . Historical argument alone cannot force anyone to believe that Jesus was raised from the dead; but historical argument is remarkably good at clearing away the undergrowth behind which scepticisms of various sorts have been hiding. The proposal that Jesus was raised bodily from the dead possesses unrivalled power to explain the historical data at the heart of Christianity.[42]

A HERMENEUTIC OF LOVE

As a committed Christian myself, I am intrigued by Carnley's proposal that the *event* of the resurrection could be identified with the Presence of Jesus in the sacramental life of the church (the "High Church" version of Bultmann's identification of the resurrection with the earliest Christian proclamation), but I would prefer to somehow retain respect for the Gospels' testimony to the historical eventfulness of the resurrection of Jesus and identify the *subject* of the resurrection, that is, the *person* of the risen Jesus, with the Presence in the sacramental life of the church. While I am inclined to agree with Richard Swinburne that the resurrection of Jesus will only be considered a matter of historical research if belief in God otherwise makes sense to the historian, I am hopeful that what I have dubbed the "Third Millennium" approach to history—one that does not firewall history off from philosophy and theology—is in fact taking hold, as a pragmatic and constructive alternative to the paralysis of postmodernism, allowing for mutual *respect* if not agreement among historians employing different metaphysical schema. I am grateful for Schüssler Fiorenza's introduction of the literary mode of *testimony*, which places the onus on those holding the revisionist understanding of the resurrection to explain the co-existence of the traditions of the appearances and the empty tomb rather than presume the mythological development of an originally unvarnished, non-miraculous, "historical" core. I am also grateful for Frei's description of narrative modes of subject-manifestation and subject-alienation. Both Frei and Schüssler Fiorenza maintain that, as testimony, the Gospel narratives do

42. Ibid., 717–18.

not "prove" that Jesus was raised from the dead, but, given what we have discussed, does any historical reconstruction prove anything? Even in law, convictions that are "beyond a reasonable doubt" are occasionally overturned. Because history is by definition non-repeatable, it doesn't admit of the same kind of proof that scientific experiments in physics, chemistry, and to some extent biology do.

As the heir to much of this discussion, Scot McKnight dares to ask his colleagues how it is that historians and biblical scholars are so *systematically* suspicious of the New Testament texts that refer to the resurrection of Jesus when they obviously represent a confluence of independent traditions and exceed the burden of proof placed on other ancient texts that are accepted as having historical value. He invites his fellow scholars to approach the New Testament in the same grateful and appreciative manner they approach other texts, using what he calls a "hermeneutic of love." This hermeneutic offers the benefit of the doubt—to a point; it genuinely "trusts the word of others" as authentic until there is reason to believe otherwise, and resists the temptation on the part of "the Subject (reader) to swallow up the Object in his or her own ideological agenda." At best, even when facing the prospect of having to declare something inauthentic, a hermeneutic of love searches for ways to believe a text until its efforts are exhausted; at the least, it seeks to "delay the judgement until after genuine encounter and reading of the text occur."[43] Far from arguing for special pleading for the New Testament accounts to be privileged because they are the church's "holy scripture," McKnight is asking for fair treatment. Although I would agree with him, I must admit that his idea of fairness, which I would share, is only relevant within a worldview that allows for the initial credibility of testimony to the miraculous, and that is a matter of the assumptions—literally, the predilections—of the individual historian. Admitting that the historian's subjectivity is part of history writing, but further admitting that the historian's subjectivity is itself subject to historical inquiry, is critical to the "resurrection" of history that needs to take place before the historical eventfulness of the resurrection of Jesus can be authentically investigated.

In the end, "belief"—whether it be in a historical construct or a theological construct—is a complex human phenomenon, and historians as well as theologians will do well to take into account the wide array of influences and motivations when it comes to securing agreement with any historical hypothesis and its implied worldview.

---

43. McKnight, *Jesus and His Death*, 38.

QUESTIONS FOR CONSIDERATION

Seminary

1. What do you think is the proper relationship of evidence to faith in the case of the resurrection of Jesus?
2. Should the interpretation of the New Testament testimonies to the resurrection ultimately belong to the church or to scholarship?

Study Group

1. How did you come to believe/disbelieve in the resurrection of Jesus?
2. Why do you think that some people do or do not believe in the resurrection of Jesus?

Individual

1. What is your response to Padgett's contention that faith doesn't provide existential/absolute certainty?
2. In what ways does it actually matter to you whether the resurrection is history or mythology?

7 The Resurrection of History Matters

MOST PROSE WRITING, INCLUDING history writing, is enhanced by some manageable degree of self-identification on the author's part: finding out key information about the perspective of the author often serves as that "Aha!" moment for the reader, whether the reader is motivated to uphold, dismiss, or simply comprehend the material at hand. What follows next is my best attempt to efficiently orient the reader to my own perspective, and it should come as no surprise that I do so by offering it in narrative form.

I was ordained in my mid-twenties as a Protestant minister in Canada's largest Protestant denomination. I was philosophically trained, personally energetic, and graduated at the top of my class. Although it might seem strange to some readers, some of my professional success in that context was due to my holding a thoroughly modern worldview: I believed in God, but not one who interferes with us "down here," I spoke vaguely of an afterlife, and I mined the biblical texts for the moral truths they offered. After serving local congregations for ten years in New Brunswick and Nova Scotia, I moved back to Toronto up ministerial duties at a modern, liberal local church in a mid-town, suburban community.

One day I received a telephone call from a young woman who worked at a local retirement residence. She told me the story of how one of the staff there, while giving birth to twins a couple of days previously, had taken a turn for the worse and had lapsed into a coma. The babies had been delivered by Caesarian section, but the mother was gravely ill, and the doctors had warned the family that blood tests indicated that there would likely be severe organ damage and quite possibly brain-damage. The young woman who called thought it would be nice if I could arrange some sort of prayer service to bring comfort to the other staff. I immediately agreed, and asked for the mother's name. "Manabat," I was told. I said that I didn't recognize

The Resurrection of History

that name, and she told me it was Filipino. "If she's Filipino," I said, "she's very likely Catholic. I should call over to the local parish and see if they know her." We agreed on that, so I rang up the office at the Conventual Franciscan Parish of St. Bonaventure—St. Bonnie's as it was known locally—and was connected to Friar David Suckling. After a brief conversation, we agreed that we would invite the staff and any residents that might want to come at 11:00 a.m. the day after next for a brief prayer service. I would bring a pianist, and Friar David would bring the candles, and we would sort it out on the fly. By that time, if she was still living, the woman would have been in a coma for eleven days.

When we arrived at the retirement residence we were ushered to a recreation room where the staff had gathered—along with a couple of hundred residents, replete with canes, walkers, and wheelchairs. It was quite a sight. The two Davids prayerfully took turns offering readings, hymns, and prayers for about forty-five minutes, and it all flowed together as if we had worked on it for months. The staff and residents were extremely grateful, and David and I sensed a connection between us that I am pleased to say we deepened over the years that followed. After a few afternoon duties, I made it home and was greeted by the message that Friar David had called and wanted me to call back right away. He had been summoned to the hospital after the service to see the woman we were praying for and he went immediately, fearing bad news. When he arrived, however, he was told that around 11:30 a.m. that morning (while we were conducting the prayer service), the patient had woken up, saying she was hungry! All subsequent tests indicated no permanent damage of any kind. Later interviews with the patient and the family corroborated this version of events. When I got off the phone, my wife wanted to know why Friar David was so urgent to speak with me. I remember staring sort of blankly and stammering that I may have just been involved in a miracle.

The story got around the neighborhood, but didn't cause quite as much of a stir as I might have expected. Parishioners at St. Bonnie's largely responded with, "Yeah, we've come to expect that kind of thing now and then." My own flock largely responded with an attitude of, "Huh! What a coincidence!" Now I was well aware that people lapse into comas, and many spontaneously emerge from comas, but the *timing* seemed too perfect. Allowing for the existence of God as I did, and having been influenced by Alfred North Whitehead's critique of the mechanistic model of the universe, there was at least a crack—a gap?—in my theological fortress that caused

The Resurrection of History Matters

me to muse, "Alright, Mr. (David) Hume, tell me that it is more likely that this is a coincidence than a miracle!" More than a decade later, I still have many questions about this event, such as why did *this* woman, this family, this community receive *this* miracle, while so many other situations cry out, in my mind at least, for the same kind of divine intervention. The fact that I have not neatly boxed in this event as a theological datum, however, does not allow me to exclude it from being something historical.

As I continued my ministry, preparing sermons week after week, I have to say that I would later resonate with Borg's image of "meeting Jesus again for the first time"—only the Jesus I was *now* meeting in the Gospels was a far stranger, more mysterious, more radical figure than the image that Borg presents. I found myself forced by my own experience, against the grain of my ecclesial tradition, into being more open-minded toward the surface-claims of the Gospel narratives. Ultimately, while finishing up my Doctor of Ministry, I made application to do a doctorate in systematic theology, with an interdisciplinary slant: I needed to know if what I was reading in the Gospels was in any sense *historically* true and, if so, how that might matter. This book is the culmination of that process.

WHAT IS TRUTH?

Pilate is said to have responded to Jesus' assertion of telling the truth by asking, "What is truth?" (John 18:38). In the Gospel writer's handling, this exchange was no doubt set up as a literary echo of Jesus' earlier claim to the questioning of Thomas when he said, "I am the way, the truth, and the life" (John 14:6), and it acts as perhaps the paradigmatic example of John's contention that "the world knew him not" (John 1:10). On the one hand, it seems just too poetically convenient not to have been fabricated; on the other hand, that kind of exchange might well have taken place, provoked by Jesus, if in fact the carpenter's son from Nazareth was at any time a popular prophet and ever stood before a Roman governor of Palestine whose education likely included rhetoric and philosophy. Whether or not this question was ever found on the lips of Pilate, it served John's readers well because it posed as important a question in the first century as the twenty-first.

I would suggest that in the Western philosophical tradition there have been two major concerns about the truth-value of propositions: we want to know whether or not what we say reflects objective reality (correspondence) and whether or not what we say is consistent with other things we want to say (coherence). Some statements require correspondence to have any value. For example, the statement "That book is on that table" isn't very meaningful unless reference is being made to an actual book and an actual table. Other statements call for coherence, but don't have any dimension of correspondence. For example, while the statement "a + b = c" tells you about the relationship of a and b to c, the statement doesn't necessarily tell you anything about anything that actually exists. Taking a second look at the first statement, however, we can notice that there is a necessary quality of coherence in it as well, because it only makes sense if a book is the kind of thing that *could* be on a table. The statement "the sunset is on the table," for instance, immediately raises objections, because what we mean by "sunset" and "table" don't really allow us, in the ordinary use of language, to talk about one of them being physically "on" the other, only that it could *appear* that way.

As we have seen through the lens of history writing, these two dimensions of correspondence and coherence come together in any thorough historical method. To focus exclusively on the dimension of coherence without reference to objective reality leaves us in postmodernism's hall of mirrors: statements are only true in relation to other statements. To focus exclusively on a "foundation of facts" without reference to those concepts that allow us to assert statements as "factual" leaves us unable to prioritize our observations on the basis of relevance: we see but do not see, we hear but do not understand. All sensible history writing, it seems, relies on the kind of blended epistemology for which Susan Haack coined the term *foundherentism*.[1] Likening these two dimensions to the "across" and "down" clues of a crossword puzzle, Haack says that we use coherence to critique, correct, and confirm factual foundations, and we use foundational facts to critique, correct, and confirm the conditions of coherence. In the case of historical inquiry, historical reconstructions can and must function according to both dimensions. All historical reconstructions can be further and further analyzed into their constituent elements, with all of these elements in turn analyzed for their reliability (correspondence) and their consistency (coherence), *ad infinitum*. At some point, however, the historian is called on to stop and *judge* that we have sufficient grounds to declare something historical.

In the case of the resurrection of Jesus, as in all other historical hypotheses, many foundational facts require certain specified conditions of

---

1. Haack, *Evidence and Inquiry*.

coherence, and many specified conditions of coherence require certain foundational facts. Among the most important conditions of coherence are (a) the concern of ancient writers for factuality; (b) the likely meaning of "resurrection" for first-century writers; (c) the general credibility of overlapping, non-identical accounts; and (d) the admissibility of non-analogous events into the historical record. Among the most important foundational facts are (1) the attestation of multiple sources; (2) the specific claims of the relevant documents; (3) the relative weakness of counter-claims; and (4) the emergence of the early church.

I think that we have dealt sufficiently with most of these if our end is to argue that the resurrection of Jesus is something that can be argued for on historical grounds. While ancient writers may have dealt with different concerns from contemporary authors, their concern for historical truth was real. The meaning of "resurrection" for first-century Jewish writers was in fact eschatological, and not natural (in the sense of being the predictable product of a confluence of existing conditions), which excludes the resurrection of Jesus from other known categories, such as resuscitation or merely visionary appearances. The lack of homogenization of the details of the resurrection narratives suggests a fidelity to originating accounts, rather than the stylized development of a grand myth. And the admissibility of events without perfect analogy is simply a function of historical events being the product of human and divine freedom, and not entirely the necessary products of existing historical forces. The distinctness of the Gospel narratives from the appearance narratives, as well as the distinctness of the Markan, Matthean, Lukan, and Johanine treatments, allows the reader of the New Testament to infer multiple sources of information that can be read as corroborative rather than conspiratorial. The claims made by the authors of the New Testament, when not dismissed out of hand, indicate a single emergence of Jesus of Nazareth from the tomb in which he was laid, and a series of appearances to his disciples that was considered by them to be both comforting and frightening, and altogether unexpected. Counter-claims that the empty tomb was a hoax or a fraud cannot produce a convincing account of motive on the part of any known or conjectured party. And the dominant emphasis of the resurrection of Jesus in the earliest-known proclamation of the church indicates that this was not a later outgrowth of tradition but rather that the resurrection of Jesus was the catalyst for the entire Christian movement.

The Resurrection of History

In completing a crossword puzzle, it is entirely possible at some points to fill in the wrong words and yet have the entire puzzle fit together. However, not all possible answers fit the matrix of clues as well as others. Neither the "across" clues nor the "down" clues in themselves ultimately prove the historical veracity of the claims of the New Testament writers or of the church, but historical inquiry that does not exclude the miraculous—the wondrous, the singular, the one-off—from consideration would probably find the actual resurrection of Jesus fills in the blank left by known historical clues better than any other hypothesis advanced thus far.

REVIEWING THE RESURRECTION

Before I go on to consider a few of the theological implications of concluding that the resurrection was in fact a historical event, I want to review just what kind of event I will be talking about.

First, it is plain to me that the New Testament speaks of Jesus' resurrection as *bodily*. Mark's Gospel, almost universally understood to be the earliest of the canonical Gospels, even in its truncated account of the resurrection, emphasizes the concern that the women had over access to his body for purposes of anointing, and that they are met with the angelic declaration of the movement of the body: "He has been raised; he is not here. Look, there is the place they laid him" (Mark 16:6). Matthew echoes Mark's emphasis on the bodily nature of the resurrection, stating that the disciples "took hold of his feet" (Matt 28:9), and affirming that the attempt to squelch tales of Jesus' resurrection has to do with the absence of his body: "You must say, 'His disciples came by night and stole him away while we were asleep'" (v. 13). Luke depicts the risen Jesus as literally walking with two disciples to the town where they were staying (Luke 24:15), and literally breaking bread with them (v. 30). Luke also quotes Jesus as having said to another gathering of disciples, "Why are you frightened, and why do doubts arise in your hearts? Look at my hands and feet; see that it is I myself. Touch me and see, for a ghost does not have flesh and bones as you see that I have" (v. 38–39). He even asked for fish and "ate in their presence" as if to underline for them that he was still *human* (v. 42–43). The same author, writing in the book of Acts, says that Jesus "presented himself alive to the by many convincing proofs, appearing to them during forty days and speaking about the kingdom of God" (Acts 1:3). These *appearances* of Jesus were not, according to Luke, different in nature from his walking, talking, and eating with them; there is nothing here to suggest that these were supplemental, visionary experiences were similar in kind to the later appearances to Paul. John carries the same concern for the empty tomb as the other evangelists, and reports Jesus as having said to Mary, "Do not hold on to me" (John 20:17), and inviting Thomas to touch the wounds still visible in his hands and in his side (v. 24–29). In the supplementary chapter to his Gospel, John reports that Jesus handled food and walked with Peter.

What can be noted with some interest is that the New Testament narratives, when presented in the order that most contemporary scholars date their writing, show no evidence of increasing emphasis on the corporeality of Jesus' resurrection, even if the effect of listing the distinctive descriptions of Jesus' resurrection-form offers us further details, perhaps in response to emerging questions from the faith community. While there is no evidence to suggest that the Christians had become embarrassed by this claim—it would be reaffirmed by the earliest church fathers—it is more likely to be the case that the matter was taken as firmly established, at least until the church grew large enough to have its teachings publicly challenged. The *earliest* canonical traditions emphasize the bodily nature of the resurrection most clearly; if there is development in the tradition, it is not toward conceiving of the resurrection as bodily, but rather of thematically developing the implications of the bodily resurrection of Jesus for those in the community of faith.

Second, it is plain to me that the New Testament speaks of Jesus' resurrection as a single *event*. While it is true that Paul's first letter to the Corinthians is the earliest written record of the resurrection that we now possess, Paul, for all the independence of the other apostles that he claims for himself elsewhere (e.g., Gal 1:11—2:14), here rests his case entirely on earlier tradition that had been formed and offered to him: "For I handed onto you as of first importance what I in turn had received" (1 Cor 15:3). Exactly what Paul had received in total and from whom is lost from the historical record, but the similarities in wording in 1 Corinthians and Luke's Gospel suggests that there was some dependence of one on the other, or perhaps both of them depend on common oral or written sources. If this is true, it takes some wind out of the sails of those who posit that what Paul calls "appearances" are qualitatively different from the events reported in the Gospels, for which Luke uses the same word. Even if we discount this, we can note that Paul's references to the resurrection *appearances* of Jesus in 1 Corinthians are clearly predicated on the *eventfulness* of the death and

The Resurrection of History

resurrection of Jesus: "that Christ dies for our sins in accordance with the scriptures, and that he was buried, and that he was raised on the third day in accordance with the scriptures" (v. 4). In fact, Paul's model of "resurrection" here is entirely eventful. When Paul speaks of "resurrection" he is not talking about a metaphysically constant dimension of life-after-death, but a future occurrence: "For the trumpet will sound and the dead will be raised imperishable, and we will be changed" (v. 52). Jesus, having already been resurrected, is "the first fruits of those who have died" (v. 20).

The New Testament consistently and vividly connects our new life in Christ—our being "raised with Christ" (Col 3:1)—to the resurrection of Jesus. Sometimes the suggestion is made that our "having been raised" is the same as Jesus' "having been raised." As intriguing and as fruitful as this may be theologically, there is a temporal condition imposed on us that is not imposed on Jesus: for all that we are *now* raised, there is a coming day when we *will be* raised, something which is never said of Jesus. Our identification with Jesus means that we are spiritually raised with Jesus, that our life is bound up with his, but this does not preclude a future resurrection that still awaits us: "but we ourselves, who have the first fruits of the Spirit, groan inwardly while we wait for adoption, the redemption of our bodies" (Rom 8:23). Other New Testament writers echo this, such as the author of the first letter of John: "What we will be has not yet been revealed. What we do know is this: when he is revealed, we will be like him, for we will see him as he is" (1 John 3:3). The resurrection of Jesus, while often stated in terms of his glorification by God, is consistently depicted in terms of a past event that was unique to him, as in the letter to the Hebrews when its author invokes "the God of peace, who brought back from the dead our Lord, Jesus, the great shepherd of the sheep" (Heb 13:20).

Third, it is plain to me that the New Testament portrays the resurrection of Jesus as an event with *eschatological significance*. As is often pointed out, merely *identifying* Jesus' postmortem existence as "resurrection" invokes the ultimate consummation of history and the judgment of humankind. More than that, however, if the resurrection of humankind is prefigured, previewed, and primed in Jesus, how does that affect our estimate of who he is in the greater scheme of things? The New Testament is very clear throughout in proclaiming that Jesus was "declared to be Son of God with power according to the spirit of holiness by resurrection from the dead" (Rom 1:4). Matthew implies that it is at, after, through, and as a consequence of the resurrection that Jesus can say, "All authority in heaven

The Resurrection of History Matters

and earth has been given to me" (Matt 28:18). At his baptism, which for Christians became a prefiguring of Jesus' death and resurrection, God announces the fulfillment of the ancient words, "You are my Son, the Beloved; with you I am well pleased" (Mark 1:11), and these words are repeated at his transfiguration, which previewed his resurrection-glory (Luke 9:35). The apocalyptic vision that concludes the traditional New Testament canon depicts Jesus as saying, "Do not be afraid; I am the first and the last, and the living one. I was dead, and see I am alive forever and ever; and I have the keys of Death and Hades" (Rev 1:17–18).

The reported exchanges between Jesus and his disciples about his upcoming arrest, crucifixion, and resurrection are very often evaluated as the invention of the evangelist(s), but there may be a more straightforward explanation that extends a "hermeneutic of love" to the Gospels. It is no stretch of the imagination for Jesus to have surmised that his prophetic ministry, undertaken in the spirit of Elijah and in succession to John the Baptist, would end in his death at the hands of the authorities. As one who sided firmly with the Pharisees against the Sadducees in his teaching about the resurrection of the dead (Matt 22:23–33), as one who saw himself one day being unjustly martyred for the sake of the nation, predicting his resurrection on "the third day" may well have been understood by his disciples as meaning that Jesus was confident he would be ultimately vindicated, as would the nation: "After two days he will revive us; on the third day he will raise us up, that we may live before him" (Hos 6:2). In my more speculative moments, not knowing what *Jesus* did and did not know, I can't help but wonder in light of his denials (Mark 13:32) how much Jesus actually knew about how and when God would fulfill the ancient prophecies in him. Was Jesus as initially surprised as the disciples that God had raised him *in* history rather than at the *end* of history? How much human thought did Jesus require to comprehend what God had done for him, in him, and through him? At any rate, if Jesus *did* speak of his future resurrection to his disciples, this may have helped them categorize his postmortem existence as resurrection. Those who deny the bodily, eventful resurrection of Jesus are forced to import alien categories into first-century Jewish-Christian thinking to make sense of New Testament claims regarding the resurrected Jesus, and/or to deny the consistency of the later narratives with the earlier correspondence, as if the narratives had illegitimately "concretized" the once-spiritual proclamation of Jesus' exaltation. Allowing the New Testament claims to stand as within the realm of possibility allows for the discernment of a much more coherent system of thought among the letters, narratives and the apocalypse than is otherwise possible.

BUT CAN IT REALLY BE TRUE?

As we have been discussing, with the help of historians, philosophers, and theologians, whether or not the bodily, eventful, eschatological resurrection of Jesus could actually be historical depends on certain conditions. In Western Christianity, there seems to be two dominant theological schemes. Though I will not hide my preference for the orthodox view, I will try to represent each of them fairly and not overblow the contrast.

The first theological scheme is *theism* (from *theos*, Greek for "god"). Theism construes God as an infinite source of being, distinct from the universe which depends on God for its existence. Most traditional forms of theism speak mythically about God creating the universe *ex nihilo* (I say "mythically" because even theologians cannot explain how God might act before the creation of time). Most contemporary theistic theologians speak of divine *kenosis*, a process by which God partially withdraws the divine attributes in such a way that something which is *not* God can exist. The universe is not isolated from God, but God remains connected to all existence, and God can be said to be "in" all things. In the theistic scheme, God is conceived of as *supra-personal*, possessing but transcending all the attributes of that which identifies us as personal, such as thought, will, freedom, and so on. Since God's internal processes are not limited as ours are, we properly speak of divine attributes *analogously*, that is, God's joy is *like* our joy, but infinitely greater, richer, purer, etc. Most Christian theology speaks of God as omnipresent, omniscient, omnipotent, and omnibenevolent.

This God, having created the universe as an expression of divine love, invites the universe to become conscious of its relationship to God, and cooperate with God, each element according to its potential. Humanity, possessing the most developed consciousness within the created universe, bears a special responsibility for discovery of God and stewardship of God's creation. However, humanity in its God-given freedom does not always remain conscious of its relationship to God, and often fails to cooperate with God, and does not live up to its full potential. God, in inexhaustible love, reaches out to humanity time and again, in ways that offer critical guidance while respecting humanity's freedom: God "inspires" poets, prophets, and political leaders, and offers us enduring touchstones, among which the

Jews prize the *Torah*, Christians prize the Gospel, and Muslims prize the Quran. Humanity in turn, having received such guidance, responds with ritual devotion and its best efforts to emulate divine standards of mercy and justice in its private and societal living. Most theists believe that through these historical revelations they have received promises or at least hints of continued human existence beyond natural death.

The second theological scheme is *deism* (from *deus*, Latin for "god"). Deism also construes God as an infinite source of being, distinct from the universe which depends on God for its existence. Most forms of deism speak philosophically about God creating the universe as a direct reflection of divine qualities, using the language of cause and effect rather than intention. The universe is not isolated from God, but the universe is created with its own powers, principles, and potentials, and God's character can be said to be reflected in all things. In the deistic scheme, God is conceived of as *non-personal*, reflected more in the constancy and power of scientific principles rather than in the variability of human characteristics. Since God's internal processes are reflected in the structure of the universe, and the universe obviously works according to rational order, we can infer that God is to be identified with reason. Many deists can therefore speak of God being omnipresent, omniscient, omnipotent, and perhaps even omnibenevolent, but never as acting spontaneously: God can do, and does, whatever is consistently reasonable for God to do.

This God, having created or emanated the universe as an expression of divine wisdom, passively invites the universe to become conscious of its relationship to God, and cooperate with God, each element according to its potential. Humanity, possessing the most developed consciousness within the created universe, bears a special responsibility for discovery of God and stewardship of God's creation. However, humanity in its God-given freedom does not always remain conscious of its relationship to God, and often fails to cooperate with God, and does not live up to its full potential. God's wisdom remains constant, however, and the universal revelation of God's mind is ever and always available to everyone in equal measure, without God having to intervene in the course of events, which would be self-contradictory for God. Humanity at its best responds to God's self-revelation in the created order by aspiring to the ideas of mercy and justice in its private and societal living. Deists for the most part are agnostic about life after death, but call for courage in the face of the certainty of death.

The Resurrection of History

Having covered the ground we've covered, it seems possible to connect these theological schemes to the "orthodox" and "revisionist" views of the resurrection of Jesus outlined at the beginning of this treatment. The orthodox view of the resurrection can be construed as a foundational fact that is coherent within a theistic Christian theology. The revisionist view of the resurrection can be construed as a foundational fact coherent within a deistic Christian theology. Although it would be rather unfair of me to do any more than conjecture, it seems fairly clear that there is a fundamental divide between those who preclude the possibility of the bodily, eventful resurrection of Jesus by reason of working within a modernist or deistic framework and those who entertain the possibility of the bodily, eventful resurrection of Jesus by reason of working within a theistic framework using a third-millennium historical methodology. Though not all of them would say that they were theologizing, and many would claim to be operating as theologically neutral historians, we have seen that is an ultimately impossible claim. While members of both sets of academic inquirers were willing to explore the *significance* of the resurrection of Jesus, they would naturally come to frame their *theological* conclusions with a view to coherence within their worldviews.

In *The Gospel in a Pluralistic Society*,[2] Lesslie Newbiggin identifies how all persons live within "plausibility structures." These structures are made up of beliefs, opinions, relationships, and personal feelings. They are more or less systematic views of the world into which new information may or may not fit. Introduction of new conceptual elements typically provokes resistance on our part; incorporation of new conceptual elements may require the restructuring of our mental worlds, work that is not usually undertaken lightly. If one has highly systematic, Westernized views on medicine and medical practice, for instance, a scientifically reliable study purporting to show the efficacy of acupuncture might cause consternation. On the other hand, if one has little interest in political history or gender politics, a new hypothesis suggesting that Elizabeth I of England was actually a man would be of little impact. In the case of the resurrection of Jesus, the energy and inventiveness of those who want to remain in dialogue with the New Testament or the Christian tradition is something at which to marvel: many will seem unwilling to concede that their deistic (or perhaps agnostic or atheistic) frames of reference simply cannot accommodate the claims of the early Christians in regards to the resurrection of Jesus.

---

2. Newbiggin, *Gospel in a Pluralistic Society*.

The Resurrection of History Matters

These claims only make sense within a theistic framework. Immediately, they are at least capable of being entertained by theists; non-Christian theists may beg to differ with Christian claims as to the theological significance of the resurrection of Jesus, but our common frames of reference could at least give rise to meaningful historical debate. These claims *could* make sense to those whose plausibility structures did not have a strongly held concept of God to begin with: though it might be rare, one could conceive how someone could, sorting through the historical arguments, conclude that Jesus had been raised from the dead and thereby be motivated to *adopt* a theistic frame of reference. For those with strongly held deistic frame of reference, the bodily, historically eventful resurrection of Jesus is simply a non-starter; rather than vilify them for being inept historians, we might more charitably conclude that they are excellent historians working in a different frame of reference.

For my part, I am a committed theist. I recognize that I am inclined to hold opinions on subjects that seem to me to be consistent with a theistic belief in God. My deepest friendships are typically (though there are exceptions) with those who share my beliefs. I feel *personally* connected to God through public and private religious devotion. Being a theist commits me, I believe, to honoring God above all else, even if in practice I do so rather poorly. I perhaps echo the best instincts of Karl Barth here by saying if we are going to talk about God, let's talk about *God*. In my poor mind, a God who is alive, active, self-aware, and able to relate personally is in all these respects superior to a god who cannot. I find the theistic vision of God to reflect a Being (if I can call God that, at least for the moment) superior to the God of deism.

To refer to God as supra-personal (or Personal with a capital "P") may well be dismissed by many in our day and age as a romantic notion. Almost anything these days can be dismissed by being labeled "romantic," as if romantic were a synonym for delusional, but I remain unapologetically romantic. I believe the universe was created in love, and that we love truth because truth leads us back to God, our ultimate Lover. I do not think that being a romantic necessitates my being a fuzzy thinker. Perhaps, as is much the thesis of *The Master and His Emissary: The Divided Brain and the Making of the Western World*,[3] being a romantic may make me an *integrative* thinker. Through the twentieth century the scientific world has made huge advances, both at the "low end" of unraveling the chemical coding of the hu-

---

3. McGilchrist, *Master and His Emissary*.

man genome, and the "high end" of relativity theory. If one can characterize this progress in terms of large-scale frameworks, the universe is looking less and less like a mechanism and more and more like an ecosystem, even an organism. Our basic models for existence are dynamic rather than static, admitting of a certain kind of fundamental freedom that may be far more frightening to contemplate than the relatively safe confines of predictable machinery. If anyone wants to categorically object to the admissibility of a supra-personal God into the plausibility structure in which science or, more to our subject matter, history is concerned, he or she may be in for a very bad twenty-first century. Nevertheless, from this point forward, as I begin to unpack some of the theological implications of concluding that the resurrection of Jesus was a bodily, eventful, eschatological, and therefore (in the third-millennium approach to historical inquiry) *historical* event, I stand with New Testament scholar Raymond Brown as he calls his fellow Christians to remember that

> the modern world view is no more infallible than the first-century world view—it knows more about some things but is less perceptive in other ways. Our generation must be obedient, as were our predecessors, to what *God* has chosen to do in Jesus; and we cannot impose on the picture what we think God should done.[4]

SHARING RESURRECTION FAITH TODAY

It is one thing for me to establish the conditions and relative credibility of proclaiming the historical resurrection of Jesus as bodily, eventful, and eschatological; it is another thing to indicate what difference it might make. These concluding paragraphs are my attempt to indicate ways in which the orthodox view of the resurrection—in contrast with the revisionist view—makes a profound difference facing profound new questions arising in the closing centuries of the second millennium and sure to be a staple of life in the third millennium.

---

4. Brown, *Virginal Conception and Bodily Resurrection of Jesus*, 72.

The Resurrection of History Matters

In a world that is interconnected by new communication technologies and migrations of peoples on a scale never seen before, how does Christian faith address people of other perspectives and faiths?

Anthony Godzieba, in symposium with Lieven Boeve and Michele Saracino, stresses that the resurrection of Jesus is and can only be the resurrection of "this finite concrete being, this contingent being, who remains in all eternity."[5] Against the Enlightenment and deistic tendency to see the specificity of Jesus as exemplary of more general, abstract truth, they argue that the Christian proclamation by its very *nature* depends on specificity and particularity—in a word, *embodiment*:

> One cannot ignore the fact that belief in Christ's bodily resurrection stands at the beginning of Christianity, and belief in the resurrection of our bodies stands at the "end." These defining moments form an *inclusion* that structures all Christian life and is the reason for Christianity fundamental commitment to Incarnation and sentimentality.[6]

Godzieba contends, in agreement with Brown, that the bodily nature of the resurrection of Jesus historicizes God's purposes with humanity, characterizing our "new creation" not as the destruction of our historical selves and replacing them but rather as the *transformation* of our *enduring* selves. Further, by using—and in fact, stretching—the language of corporeality to depict the resurrected Jesus, the resurrection takes up one of the key theological implications of the incarnation. "The recognition and celebration of the capacity of the material and the particular to mediate divine presence." In other words, "*the grammar of the Resurrection is the intensification of the grammar of Incarnation.*"[7]

The *truth* of Jesus' teachings only becomes actualized by their incarnation in Jesus' life and actions; further, that actualization did not take place in "an all-purpose, generic, one-size-fits-all human nature," but rather in the specificity of a particular human life. Godzieba deplores any attempt to conceive of Christianity as one more therapeutic player in the human potential movement, as if Christian faith could be reduced to what we *distil and universalize* from Jesus' life. The particularity of Jesus' life, continued

5. Godzieba et al., "Resurrection—Interpretation—Transformation," 778.
6. Ibid., 784.
7. Ibid., 788.

in the bodily transformation of resurrection, implies the recognition and celebration of the particular concreteness of the life of each one of Jesus' followers. Moreover, the vulnerability of God's self-incarnation, made permanent in the resurrection of Jesus, implies a continuing vulnerability in the ongoing living-out of Jesus' proclamation. Somewhere between the extremes of regarding language as non-referential and naively believing in a universal viewpoint is a "post-postmodern Christian humanism" that emphasizes "the essential role that embodiment plays . . . to promote human flourishing."[8]

Building on Godzieba's observations, Boeve admits that "the ongoing defense of Jesus Christ as the ultimate expression of the core of the Christian faith remains a problem for continuing dialogue with other religions and convictions."[9] Boeve rejects the option of pluralism that relativizes Christian truth claims on the one hand, and the Rahnerian "anonymous Christian" option that is in fact a cloaked exclusivism on the other. While pluralism makes Christianity representative of the universal, exclusivism identifies itself with the universal—and both fail to comprehend the full significance of the particularity of the incarnation and resurrection. Recalling that there is no "bird's-eye view" of the world, and that Christians must view other religious perspectives from the particularity of their own Christian perspective, Boeve calls for a "different inclusivism" in which Christians enter into interreligious dialogue aware of the particularity of the *content* of our faith as well as the particularity of the *mode* of our faith.

Boeve challenges reigning Western epistemology that sees the universal as the *real* repository of truth. For Christians, truth is ultimately revealed in the "concrete humanity" of Jesus: "After his death, his disciples confess this same Jesus: that he had risen, and that he was the Christ, God's Son *in* his humanity and not *in spite* of it. The one who desires to know God must look at Jesus."[10] Confessing that all understandings of God's revelation in Jesus are themselves particular and contingent does not invalidate them, but may rather be taken together as indicative of God's desire to be incarnate in the contingent and particular. Boeve goes on to say that the centrality of the resurrection to Christian faith "confirms and supplements the theological-epistemological link between incarnation and truth," inasmuch as

---

8. Ibid., 795.
9. Ibid., 796.
10. Ibid., 805.

the Resurrection is accessible only through a hermeneutics of testimony, an auto-implicative witnessing. . . . In the Resurrection, Jesus who died for us is risen, opening for us historical human beings, embedded in particular histories, a future beyond death—not by lifting us out of this particularity or undoing it, but by healing and transforming it into life in all its fullness.[11]

Responding to both Godzieba and Boeve, Saracino commends the lifting up of embodiment as an interpretive key in exploring the meaning of the resurrection, but she asks Godzieba if he is willing to see this emphasis on particularity and embodiment through to the end: "Could black, womanist, feminist, mujerista, and queer theologians use [this] framework to speak of their own particularity, or is there something more purposely open about Godzieba's theology? . . . Put differently, what does a 'post-postmodern' embodied person imagined by Godzieba's 'post-postmodern theological anthropology' look like?"[12] And while she applauds Boeve's move to eliminate both the practice of Christians making "transcultural universal, and death-dealing claims" against people of other faiths and the practice of "watering down one's own religious particularity in order to embrace the other," she encourages both Godzieba and Boeve to walk with their fellow Christians that have been called on "to move beyond their comfort zones . . . asking them to engage in interreligious dialogue, much like Jesus' disciples did, who encountered the empty tomb and resurrected Lord with both a certainty of their love for him and openness to finding out where that love might lead them."[13]

I would be so bold as to say that connecting the *bodily* nature of the resurrection of Jesus to the dimension of its *particularity* is of no value unless that connection is contextualized within a particular community. An unqualified emphasis on the particularity of the incarnation, especially coupled with the confirming/validating impact of the resurrection of Jesus, would leave us in an atomistic fog, where every particular is as valuable as any other just because it is particular. That would leave us with no criteria for evaluating the relative merits of anything, and would, ironically, be the very kind of identifying truth with universals that Godzieba, Boeve, and Saracino are arguing against. At the other extreme, the particularity of Jesus could be broken down into characteristics and we could reason that God is

---

11. Ibid., 807.
12. Ibid., 811–12.
13. Ibid., 814.

self-revealed only in first-century Jewish males, but this process of abstraction would be, in its own fashion, another kind of identifying truth with universals such as "Jewishness" or "maleness." When contextualized by community, however, both of these extremes are avoided: *this* Jesus acted in *this* fashion when confronted by *these* circumstances, and in *that* fashion when confronted by *those* circumstances.

Some abstraction is inevitable, and not necessarily evil; for instance, because Jesus was (in his day) radically inclusive in his sense of community, Paul could later declare that in the church women would not be thought as of lesser value than men, Gentiles than Jews, even slaves than free citizens. The *historical* particularity of Jesus, however, allows us to "forgive" Jesus for not offering clear, abiding guidance on gay marriage, veganism, or the appropriate use of Facebook. Saracino rightly asks what forms of particularity will be regarded as potentially incarnational: while it may seem obvious that the particular color of one's skin can be celebrated as a gift, it is doubtful that particular degrees of sociopathy can be, and there are many other particularities, both innate and socialized, that can be the subject of furious and honest debate. Still, asking the question of whether or not any given particularity is or is not consistent with the particularity of God's self-revelation in Jesus is a worthy one to ask because (a) it drives us to constant reflection on the particular life of Jesus, and (b) it has the potential to expand our particular culture-bound views of what it means to follow Jesus.

In a world that now assumes that the universe as we know it is billions of years old and that humankind evolved from lower forms of life, how does Christian faith address the new paradigms of cosmic and human evolution?

John F. Haught reminds us that through the centuries, "Christian theology spoke of three dimensions of God's creative activity: original creation (*creatio originalis*), ongoing or continuous creation (*creatio continua*), and new creation of the fulfillment of creation (*creatio nova*)."[14] In a theistic framework, there is room for God's meaningful participation in the cosmic process between the "original" past and the "end" of the world. Given the traditional Christian metanarrative involving creaturely freedom and God's

---

14. Haught, *God after Darwin*, 37.

loving call to us, "we should logically foresee, rather than be surprised, that God's creation is not driven coercively, that it is widely experimental, and that it unfolds over the course of a considerable amount of time."[15] Including non-human elements within the scope of creaturely freedom, Haught points out, is no more anthropomorphic than standard evolutionary theory: "The explanatory success of Darwinian biology, [Richard] Dawkins insinuates, has occurred *because* of, not in spite of, its reliance on foggy yet illuminating metaphors such as 'adaptation,' 'cooperation,' 'competition,' 'survival,' and 'selection.'"[16] Since Christian faith is not deterministic, it allows for the genuinely new, and permits divine involvement as ingredient to the historical process.

Within this context, there is no theological impediment to construing Jesus' bodily, eventful resurrection as uniquely willed by God, approachable in the traditional theological terms as the exceptional self-revealing action of God. However, Haught speaks of *our* resurrection not as a reemergence of our human, bodily existence, but rather in incorporeal and amorphous terms of "a deeper relationship to the cosmos occurring in our own death [that] would not be a distancing from, but a movement toward deeper intimacy with, and eternally embodied deity."[17] In Haught's theology, the resurrection of Jesus thus serves to illustrate an eternal truth about the relationship of the universe to God, but only abstractly: even if the orthodox view of the resurrection of Jesus is upheld, it is not the truth of our destiny, but only an illustration of the principle involved. In this move, it seems apparent that Haught has decided to take the metaphysical vision of process theology's panentheism as the interpretive key to reality, in stark contrast with the move of Godzieba, Boeve, and Saracino to take the particularity of Jesus as the interpretive key.

James Cone also sees value in asserting the freedom of God in terms of the world's ongoing process, but is suspicious of attempts to align the gospel with existing metaphysical frameworks. Rather, Cone upholds the eventfulness of the resurrection of Jesus from the particular vantage point of African American oppression. He sees the very framing of the relationship between faith and history as something problematic to be characteristic of political oppressors "defending the intellectual status of religious assertions

---

15. Ibid., 42.
16. Ibid., 90.
17. Ibid., 162.

The Resurrection of History

against erosion by historical criticism."[18] Eschewing philosophically respectable frameworks, Cone argues that Jesus is properly understood as the successor to other historical liberators such as Moses and defenders of the oppressed such as Daniel. Theology should spring from Jesus' historical particularity: "Jesus was not simply a nice fellow who happened to like the poor. Rather his actions have their origin in God's eternal being. They represent a new vision of divine freedom, climaxed with the cross and resurrection, wherein God breaks into history for the liberation of slaves from societal oppression."[19]

On the other hand, Cone criticizes what he takes to be the *complete* historicization of the resurrection of Jesus by Pannenberg. In Cone's view, Panneberg goes too far in the direction of Western respectability in conceding that present experience of Jesus cannot ultimately be safeguarded against the accusation of being mere subjective illusion. Cone insists that it is precisely the *present experience* of the Holy Spirit among Black Christians that functions not as the confirmation of theology but as the *starting point* of theology. For Cone, this is not an academic discussion of hermeneutics; this is the historical foundation of Black Christian hope:

> Without the resurrection, Jesus was just a good man who suffered like other oppressed people. There is no reason to believe that God was with Jesus and thus defeated suffering unless Jesus transcended death and is alive and present in the struggle of freedom.... The resurrection, therefore, is God breaking into history and liberating the oppressed from their present suffering, thereby opening up humanity to a divine realization beyond history.[20]

By insisting that present experience is theology's starting point, however, Cone has no need of asserting the *bodily* resurrection of Jesus, presumably because that would fix theology's starting point irrevocably *in the past*. Such a move takes Cone away from the orthodox view of the resurrection and brings him close to the revisionist view of equating *faith in the resurrection* with the eventfulness of the resurrection. Cone, however, refuses identification with the revisionist view that is captive to a Troeltschian, modernist framework because he wants to establish the freedom of God as foundational. Ultimately, from a different social position, Cone makes a move similar to that of Carnley: in refusing to permit discussion

---

18. Cone, *God of the Oppressed*, 45.
19. Ibid., 81.
20. Ibid., 175–76.

of the ontological dimension of the resurrection of Jesus, Cone winds up referring to an event that is not subject to historical criticism, and therefore has become in Cone's hands an uncontestable ideological symbol. He does so in such a way, however, that places God's activity within, not merely above or at both ends of, the historical process, which a theistic framework absolutely requires.

Joao Batista Libanio begins in the same place as Cone, in the experience of oppression, but allows for some universalization of the implications of the historical resurrection of Jesus, by distinguishing between utopianism and hope. Utopian visions are useful in critiquing the present and providing alternatives. "Hope, however, grows in much more difficult and hostile ground. Its true origin is an impossible situation in human terms, one we cannot overcome by relying on our present potential and human strength, but only on God's promises and power."[21] The reign of God is precisely that, *God's* reign, and not ours, no matter how enlightened we might think ourselves to be. That is why the resurrection, God's historical intervention, and no mere historical *vision*, is the ultimate determination of Christian hope.

For Libanio, the resurrection of Jesus is not simply an elevation of optimism or the historical inevitability of progress, but God's swearing by God's own divine faithfulness that there is a goal, a *telos*, to our human existence:

> Jesus' resurrection is the prototype, precursor, and anticipation of all resurrections. In it the end of history has already happened. It also shows that only those who give their lives for their brothers and sisters rise again. Lastly, it is the ultimate key to all revelation. The last word on history has already been said. No human power, no dictator, no ruling power will decide the final destiny of the poor. God's love raised Jesus and will raise all those he loves and who love him. Among these the poor have first place.[22]

Libanio, I think, refocuses us on the historical eventfulness of the resurrection of Jesus in a way that more fully accounts for the testimony of the New Testament, and safeguards the historical particularity of the resurrection of Jesus as the key to Christian theology.

The million dollar question, it seems to me, that Christians need to address, is along these lines: in a four-billion year-long cosmic process, how

21. Libanio, "Hope, Utopia, Resurrection," 282.
22. Ibid., 289.

The Resurrection of History

dare we say that *we*—our planet, our species, our recognizable time—are the locus of God's eternal investment by means of the incarnation and resurrection of the second person of the Trinity? How can we adopt such a particularly purposeful perspective on what seems to be the Mother of All Random Processes? If I have framed that often-unconscious and largely unentertained question in an existentially significant way, perhaps I might attack not the minor premise but the major—that is, perhaps it is time that we challenged the tenet of evolutionary faith that demands the process be regarded as random. Gerard J. Hughes points out, as other have, the sheer unlikeliness of the universe as we know it:

> A universe like ours, so far as we can tell on the basis of the scientific knowledge we have, comes as a package. . . . If the fundamental forces in our universe were even very slightly different, the substances and materials to which we are accustomed simply would not exist at all. So far as we can tell, it is absolutely not possible to make small-scale changes in the laws of physics which will leave most things much the same, with only selected differences. A radically different creation might well be possible, for all we know; but a very slightly different one seems to be highly unlikely.[23]

There is certainly some credibility, both on an intuitive level and on a philosophical level, in the notion that the world as we know it is no accident. Even hard-core, atheistic Darwinists tend to uphold the belief that human beings are somehow among the most, if not the most, sophisticated creatures served up by evolutionary processes. A Christian may find evidence of divine intention in this knowledge, but more importantly the Christian finds in the resurrection of Jesus the historical confirmation of the intuition of purposefulness to cosmic and human history that is the cornerstone of the Christian metanarrative and the foundational fact of Christian theology. A skeptic might naturally demur, but anyone, Christian or otherwise, might well ask if seeing humanity as the accidental end-product of a random process is (a) a more complete explanation of anything and (b) heuristically superior to the Christian metanarrative in terms of ethical foundations for a planet now rife with genocidal warfare and armed with the means of obliterating the biosphere.

---

23. Quoted in Mahoney, *Christianity in Evolution*, 105.

In a world that has been thoroughly democratized and engaged by global political and commercial concerns, how does Christian faith proclaim the specific presence of the resurrected Jesus in the sacramental life of the church?

William Placher references the eschatological nature of the bodily, eventful resurrection of Jesus when he says concerning the Gospel accounts: "If these witnesses are truthful, then Jesus' resurrection was not an ordinary historical event but one that transformed the whole of history."[24] The divine particularity of the resurrection of Jesus challenges all preexisting categories of time and space.

For Balthasar, historical particularity is revealing of God's selfhood. Eschewing Hegel's search for a norm of history within which Jesus would fit, Balthasar cited the Christian tradition as declaring Jesus in all his particularity to be the historical norm of all history: "Thus theology in the strict sense of the word cannot do any abstracting at all; all it can do is to display the normative shining out from the irreducible fact." Any "use of general truths, propositions and methods . . . must be careful that everything of this kind always subserves the contemplation and interpretation of the unique."[25] Though Balthasar is well acquainted with Western literature, he insists that Christian faith is not one instance of faith in general, because it is faith made unique by virtue of Jesus' uniqueness. Jesus did not offer his life as a mere *illustration* of God's love, something repeatable in principle, but could only reconcile humanity and human history "from inside; he must really take upon himself the personal and social situation of the sinner. Thus the *pro nobis* means 'in our place.'"[26]

Balthasar consistently embraces the *historicity* of our redemption, such that we are "seized at the core of our being by the resurrection of Christ from the dead. It is an event which completely re-values the whole of individual human life, as it does the whole of human history."[27] By this insistence, Balthasar is not only able to identify the historicity of the resurrection as central to our redemption, but to open the door for our participation in this redemption through historical means, namely, the sacramental life of the church. Balthasar is quite aware that the church,

---

24. Placher, *Essay in Postliberal Theology*, 60.
25. Balthasar, *Theology of History*, 21–22.
26. Balthasar, *Theo-Drama: Theological Dramatic Theory*, 3:240.
27. Balthasar and Ratzinger, *Two Say Why*, 50.

The Resurrection of History

judged by secular standards, will be found wanting: it has not lived up to the reality it proclaims. Western society, becoming increasingly organized apart from the transcendent reality that the church holds forth, declares the cleavage between history and faith to be irreconcilable. Some Protestant theologians, Balthasar says, see the historical resurrection of Jesus as the *only* eschatological incursion into present human history and therefore, in his mind, leaving the resurrection of Jesus without genuine historical effect, and therefore not fully historical. Balthasar points to the forty days between Jesus' resurrection and his ascension as the demonstration that the resurrection is not *only* eschatological, but the means by which Jesus' earthly life is made the cornerstone on which he builds his church—the community which is to endure until the end of time: "The Church, transcending history but acting as its content and its nucleus, is the ultimate gift of the Creator to human history, given to bring its own realization from within."[28]

By "ultimate" Balthasar means something more like "final" as opposed to "supreme," but still he champions the church which, while it still "mourns in exile," participates like no other human community in the "world to come." The historical resurrection of Jesus means a genuinely historical life for the church, which lives as the mystical body of the risen Jesus, and directs its prayers to God in expectation of God's actual, present guidance, seeking to embody a living reality that is greater than mere recapitulation of the past and/or an orientation to an ethical "vanishing point." The church's present actions are not merely ephemeral reflections of the *ideals* of God's reign, but the center of humanity's genuine participation in, and genuine incarnation of, that reign. In such a view the post-resurrection history of Jesus' involvement in the church by the Spirit is more than sign and symbol: it is the living, breathing inauguration of God's reign.

This understanding of the life of the church challenges both the pietist and the revisionist move toward any unadorned primitivism, which concretizes some particular distillation/reconstruction of the faith of the church in the first century. If the church is the body of the *living* Christ, of that same Jesus who was raised from the dead in our time and space, the door is open for further unfolding of the full implications of the good news that was received by first-century hearers. Later proclamations of the church are not illegitimate simply because they would be expressed in language that might be perplexing to first-century hearers. If Jesus is yet present in the temporal life of the community formed around his resurrection, and

---

28. Balthasar, *Theology of History*, 141.

not merely a datum of the past, then the development of doctrine and the adaptation of Christian witness to new linguistic and cultural parameters is to be just as much expected in the twenty-first century as it was in the first.

A recent example of this kind of adaptation in the life of the church through reflection on its origins is the result the confrontation of theological scholarship and feminism. Elisabeth Schüssler Fiorenza uses a feminist hermeneutic to reject the "malestream" scholarly consensus that the Gospel narratives surrounding the empty tomb were later, legendary accretions to an earlier "visionary" root of resurrection theology. Feminist historical reconstruction rejects "the preconstructed kyriachal discourse of women's marginality and victimization" for the "assumption of women's presence and agency."[29] She upholds the "Magdalenian" tradition of the empty tomb alongside the "Petrine," and concludes that the earliest testimonies to the resurrection of Jesus were meant to depict a bodily, eventful resurrection as the heart of the gospel itself:

> The empty tomb does not signify absence but presence: it announces the Resurrected One's presence on the road ahead, in a particular space of struggle and recognition such as Galilee. The Resurrected One is present in the "little ones," in the struggles for survival of those impoverished, hungry, tortured, and killed, in the wretched of the earth.[30]

As the body of the resurrected Jesus, the church continues to listen to Jesus through his Spirit, discovering and rediscovering the eschatological significance of the resurrection. In this case, further reflection on the primacy of the women's witness to the resurrection of Jesus will doubtless bear more fruit as the church considers the place, status, and role of women within its communal life.

If in embracing the particularity of God's self-revelation in Jesus, and the historical particularity of the resurrection of Jesus, we can embrace the particularity of our Christian faith, and stop trying to "translate" all of the church's theology and practices into terms that make us feel at ease with the world around us, pressing our language and concepts into rational, "left-brained" categories respectable to the social sciences. As Iain McGilchrist laments:

---

29. Schüssler Fiorenza, *Jesus, Miriam's Child, Sophia's Prophet*, 29.
30. Ibid., 126.

The Resurrection of History

> The Western Church has, in my view, been active in undermining itself. It no longer has the confidence to stick to its values, but instead joins the chorus of voices attributing material answers to spiritual problems. At the same time the liturgical reform movement, as always convinced that religious truths can be literally stated, has largely eroded and in some cases completely destroyed the power of metaphoric language and ritual to convey the numinous. Meanwhile there has been, as expected, a parallel movement towards the possible rehabilitation of religious practices as *utility*. Thus 15 minutes Zen meditation a day may make you more effective money broker, or improve your blood pressure, or lower you cholesterol.[31]

A little less polemically, perhaps, I would say that understanding the church as the body of the resurrected Jesus would reduce our anxiety over whether there are two sacraments or seven, and encourage us to see the entire life of the church in some very strong sense as sacramental, with the sacramental rites not as independent spells of spiritual magic but as active expressions of the fulsome, underlying reality of the church.

Finally, for those of us with the luxury of twenty centuries of hindsight, respecting the church as the body of the resurrected Jesus implies that just as the church lives in continuity with its Lord so we are called to live in continuity with the church. We do not have the religious luxury of shaking our heads and disclaiming involvement in the difficult institutional history of the church throughout the ages, or distancing ourselves from any of its present dysfunctions. In some instances, it might not be too much to say that we *hate* what we have done, but the church's historical crusades are *our* crusades, the church's historical inquisitions are *our* inquisitions, and the church's historical tolerance of oppression is *our* tolerance of oppression. Whether we are at peace with it or not, the practice of penance is *our* practice, the theology of substitutionary atonement is *our* theology, and the reverence of the Virgin is *our* reverence. Where we need to own our errors, let us own them; where we need to repent, let us repent; where we need to appreciate more deeply, let us appreciate more deeply. I have no doubt that making the effort to stand with our past will be far more spiritually enriching than falsely abstracting and absolving ourselves from it.

---

31. McGilchrist, *Master and His Emissary*, 441.

The Resurrection of History Matters

A FINAL, UNFINISHED WORD

Let me commend you for making this journey with me. I hope that by examining the art of history writing I have made clear what kind of "resurrection" historical method needs before it can examine the resurrection of Jesus. I also hope that I have been able to demonstrate under what conditions the proclamation of the bodily, eventful, and eschatological resurrection of the historical Jesus could make sense, and at least teased you with a few thought-starters about what that could mean for the academy, for the church, and for you. There have been too many names, too many quotations, too many fine-grained distinctions for the taste of most, I suspect. The discussion has at time been complex, but I hope that at certain points it has also been rich enough for you to be glad you engaged it.

Having made the great effort to wade through this material, make it count: don't let anyone, no matter how educated or sincere, tell you that "no one believes in the resurrection of Jesus anymore" or that "scholars now know what Jesus was *really* like, and it's nothing like what's in the Bible." My opinion is that people who spout those opinions are a generation behind the times, but they still get calls from well-meaning journalists for "the latest" biblical or theological scholarship. If "orthodox" is a dirty word for you, feel free to speak about the "traditional" or even "biblical" view of the resurrection, and know that the mind-altering, soul-stretching, life-changing message that Christ is risen isn't going to go away.

Signing off, I will let the last pope and the first pope have the last word on my central, radical, risky thesis:

> The *factum historicum* (historical fact) is not an interchangeable symbolic cipher for biblical faith, but the foundation on which it stands. . . . If we push this aside, Christian faith as such disappears and it is recast as some other religion. —Benedict XVI[32]

> Blessed be the God and Father of our Lord Jesus Christ! By his great mercy he has given us a new birth into a living hope through the resurrection of Jesus Christ from the dead, and into an inheritance that is imperishable, undefiled, and unfading . . .
> —1 Peter 1:3–4

---

32. Ratzinger, *Jesus of Nazareth*, xv.

The Resurrection of History

QUESTIONS FOR CONSIDERATION

Seminary

1. What use would you make of the particularity of the resurrection of Jesus?
2. How do you concur with / demur from Balthasar's understanding of the church?

Study Group

1. What other things do you think a *bodily* resurrection of Jesus might imply?
2. What have been the most helpful/offensive/significant points made in this book?

Individual

1. How has your understanding of the resurrection changed through your lifetime?
2. What questions do you still have concerning the resurrection of Jesus?

Bibliography

Appleby, Joyce, et al. *Telling the Truth about History*. New York: Norton, 1994.
Aquinas, Thomas. *Summa Theologiae*. Translated by Thomas C. Moore. New York: McGraw-Hill, 1964.
Arnal, William E., and Michel Desjardins, eds. *Whose Historical Jesus?* Waterloo, ON: Wilfrid Laurier University Press, 1997.
Babini, Ellero. "Jesus Christ: Form and Norm of Man according to Hans Urs von Balthasar." In *Hans Urs von Balthasar: His Life and Work*, edited by David L. Schindler, 221–30. San Francisco: Ignatius, 1991.
Bacon, Francis. *Novum Organum Scientiarum: Containing Rules for Conducting the Understanding in the Search of Truth; and Raising a Solid Structure of Universal Philosophy*. Translated by Peter Shaw. London: Sherwood, Neely & Jones, 1818.
Balthasar, Hans Urs von. *Theo-Drama: Theological Dramatic Theory*. Vol. 2, *The Dramatis Personae: Man in God*. San Francisco: Ignatius, 1990.
———. *Theo-Drama: Theological Dramatic Theory*. Vol. 3, *The Dramatis Personae: Persons in Christ*. San Francisco: Ignatius, 1992.
———. *A Theology of History*. San Francisco: Ignatius, 1994.
———. *The Theology of Karl Barth: Exposition and Interpretation*. San Francisco: Ignatius, 1992.
———. *Word and Revelation*. Montreal: Palm, 1964.
Barth, Karl. *Church Dogmatics*. Vol. 1, pt. 2. New York: T. & T. Clark, 1956.
———. *Church Dogmatics*. Vol. 3, pt. 2. Edinburgh: T. & T. Clark, 1960.
———. *Evangelical Theology: An Introduction*. Grand Rapids: Eerdmans, 1992.
Barthes, Roland. *Image, Music, Text*. New York: Hill & Wang, 1977.
Bauckham, Richard. *God Crucified: Monotheism and Christology in the New Testament*. Grand Rapids: Eerdmans, 1998.
———. "The God Who Raises the Dead." In *The Resurrection of Jesus Christ*, edited by Paul Avis, 136–54. London: Darton, Longman & Todd, 1993.
———. *Jesus and the Eyewitnesses: The Gospels as Eyewitness Testimony*. Grand Rapids: Eerdmans, 2006.
———. "Moltmann's Theology of Hope Revisited." *Scottish Journal of Theology* 42 (1989) 199–214.
Bayle, Pierre. *Historical and Critical Dictionary: Selections*. Translated by Richard H. Popkin. Hackett, 1991.
Bloch, Marc. *The Historian's Craft*. New York: Vintage, 1953.

Bibliography

Borg, Marcus J. *Meeting Jesus Again for the First Time*. San Francisco: HarperSanFrancisco, 1994.

Borg, Marcus J., and N. T. Wright. *The Meaning of Jesus: Two Visions*. San Francisco: HarperSanFrancisco, 2000.

Braaten, Carl E., and Roy A. Harrisville, eds. *The Historical Jesus and the Kerygmatic Christ: Essays on the New Quest of the Historical Jesus*. New York: Abingdon, 1964.

Bray, Gerald. *Biblical Interpretation Past and Present*. Downers Grove: InterVarsity, 1996.

Breisach, Ernst. *Historiography: Ancient, Medieval, and Modern*. 3rd ed. Chicago: University of Chicago Press, 2006.

Brown, Raymond E. *The Virginal Conception and Bodily Resurrection of Jesus*. Toronto: Paulist, 1973.

Bryan, Christopher. "The Resurrection of Jesus and the Problem of History: Reflections on the Third Volume of N. T. Wright's Christian Origins and the Question of God." *Sewanee Theological Review* 47 (2004) 321–37.

Buller, Cornelius A. *The Unity of Nature and History in Pannenberg's Theology*. Lanham, MD: Littlefield Adam, 1996.

Bultmann, Rudolf. *The History of the Synoptic Tradition*. San Francisco: HarperSanFrancisco, 1976.

———. *Jesus and the Word*. London: Scribner, 1934.

———. "The Primitive Christian Kerygma and the Historical Jesus." In Braaten and Harrisville, *The Historical Jesus and the Kerygmatic Christ*, 1–42.

———. *Theology of the New Testament*. London: SCM, 1955.

Burridge, R. A. *What Are the Gospels? A Comparison with Graeco-Roman Biography*. New York: Cambridge University Press, 1992.

Buttrick, George Arthur. *Christ and History*. Nashville: Abingdon, 1963.

Byrskog, Samuel. *Story as History, History as Story: The Gospel Tradition in the Context of Ancient Oral History*. Boston: Brill Academic, 2002.

Caputo, John D. "Heidegger and Theology." In *The Cambridge Companion to Heidegger*, edited by Charles B. Guignon, 326–44. New York: Cambridge University Press, 2006.

Carnley, Peter. *The Structure of Resurrection Belief*. Oxford: Clarendon, 1987.

Carr, Edward Hallett. *What Is History?* London: Macmillan, 1961.

Cavin, Robert Greg. "Is There Sufficient Evidence to Establish the Resurrection of Jesus?" In *The Empty Tomb: Jesus Beyond the Grave*, edited by Robert M. Price and Jeffrey Jay Lowder, 19–42. New York: Prometheus, 2005.

Chap, Larry. "Revelation." In *The Cambridge Companion to Hans Urs von Balthasar*, edited by Edward T. Oakes and David Moss, 11–22. New York: Cambridge University Press, 2004.

Clark, Elizabeth. *History, Theory, Text: Historians and the Linguistic Turn*. Cambridge: Harvard University Press, 2004.

Coakley, Sarah. "Is the Resurrection a Historical Event?" In *The Resurrection of Jesus Christ*, edited by Paul Avis, 93–107. London: Darton, Longman & Todd, 1993.

Cochrane, Eric. "What Is Catholic Historiography?" In *God, History, and Historians: An Anthology of Modern Christian Views of History*, edited by C. T. McIntire, 443–64. New York: Oxford University Press, 1977.

Collingwood, R. G. *The Idea of History*. Toronto: Oxford, 1935.

Colombo, Joseph A. *An Essay on Theology and History: Studies in Pannenberg, Metz, and the Frankfurt School*. Atlanta: Scholars, 1990.

Cone, James H. *God of the Oppressed*. New York: Seabury, 1975.

Bibliography

Conway, Pádraic, and Fáinche Ryan. *Karl Rahner: Theologian for the Twenty-First Century.* New York: Lange, 2010.

Conyers, A. J. *God, Hope, and History: Jürgen Moltmann and the Christian Concept of History.* Macon, GA: Mercer University Press, 1988.

Cönzelmann, Hans. "The Method of the Life-of-Jesus Research." In Braaten and Harrisville, *The Historical Jesus and the Kerygmatic Christ*, 54–68.

Craffert, Pieter F. "Did Jesus Rise Bodily from the Dead? Yes and No!" *Religion and Theology* 15 (2008) 133–53.

Craig, William Lane. *Assessing the New Testament Evidence for the Historicity of the Resurrection of Jesus.* Lewiston, NY: Mellen, 1989.

———. *The Historical Argument for the Resurrection of Jesus during the Deist Controversy.* Lewiston, NY: Mellen, 1985.

———. "Wright and Crossan on the Historicity of the Resurrection of Jesus." In Stewart, *The Resurrection of Jesus*, 139–48.

Crenshaw, James L. "Love Is Stronger than Death: Intimations of Life beyond the Grave." In *Resurrection: The Origin of a Biblical Doctrine*, edited by James H. Charlesworth et al., 53–78. New York: T. & T. Clark, 1996.

Crossan, John Dominic. *The Historical Jesus: The Life of a Mediterranean Peasant.* San Francisco: HarperSanFrancisco, 1991.

Daley, Brian E. "A Hope for Worms: Early Christian Hope." In *Resurrection: Theological and Scientific Assessments*, edited by Ted Peters et al., 136–64. Grand Rapids: Eerdmans, 2002.

Davaney, Sheila Greeve. *Historicism: The Once and Future Challenge for Theology.* Minneapolis: Fortress, 2006.

D'Costa, Gavin, ed. *Resurrection Reconsidered.* Rockport, MA: OneWorld, 1996.

Denton, Donald L., Jr. *Historiography and Hermeneutics in Jesus Studies: An Examination of the Work of John Dominic Crossan and Ben F. Meyer.* London: T. & T. Clark, 2004.

Derrida, Jacques. *Dissemination.* Chicago: University of Chicago Press, 1983.

———. *Of Grammatology.* Baltimore: Johns Hopkins University Press, 1976.

———. *Positions.* Chicago: University of Chicago Press, 1981.

———. *Writing and Difference.* Chicago: University of Chicago Press, 1978.

Dickens, W. T. "Balthasar's Biblical Hermeneutics." In *The Cambridge Companion to Hans Urs von Balthasar*, edited by Edward T. Oakes and David Moss, 175–86. New York: Cambridge University Press, 2004.

Droysen, Johann Gustav. *Grundriss der Historik.* Leipzig: Veit, 1875.

Dufour, Xavier Leon. *Resurrection and the Message of Easter.* London: Chapman, 1974.

Dulles, Avery. *The Craft of Theology: From Symbol to System.* New York: Crossroad, 1996.

Dunn, James D. G. *Jesus Remembered.* Grand Rapids: Eerdmans, 2006.

Eitel, Adam. "The Resurrection of Jesus Christ: Karl Barth and the Historicization of Being." *International Journal of Systematic Theology* 10 (2008) 36–53.

Elton, G. R. *The Practice of History.* New York: Crowell, 1967.

Evans, C. F. *Resurrection and the New Testament.* London: SCM, 1970.

Evans, Craig A. *Fabricating Jesus: How Modern Scholars Distort the Gospels.* Downers Grove: InterVarsity, 2006.

Evans, Richard J. *In Defence of History.* London: Granta, 1997.

Feierman, Steven. "Africa in History: The End of Universal Narratives." In *After Colonialism: Imperialism Histories and Postcolonial Displacements*, edited by Gyan Prakash, 40–65. Princeton: Princeton University Press, 1995.

Bibliography

Fergusson, David A. "Interpreting the Resurrection." *Scottish Journal of Theology* 38 (1985) 287–305.

Foucault, Michel. *The Archaeology of Knowledge*. New York: Barnes & Noble, 1993.

———. "What Is an Author?" In *Michel Foucault: Language, Counter-Memory, Practice; Selected Essays and Interviews*, edited by Donald F. Bouchard, 113–38. Ithaca, NY: Cornell University Press, 1977.

Frederickson, Paula. "What Does Jesus Have to Do with Christ? What Does Knowledge Have to Do with Faith? What Does History Have to Do with Theology?" In *Christology: Memory, Inquiry, Practice*, edited by Anne M. Clifford and Anthony J. Godzieba, 3–17. Maryknoll: Orbis, 2003.

Frei, Hans W. *The Eclipse of the Biblical Narrative: A Study in Eighteenth and Nineteenth Century Hermeneutics*. New Haven: Yale University Press, 1974.

———. "How It All Began: On the Resurrection of Christ." *Anglican and Episcopal History* 58 (1989) 139–45.

———. *The Identity of Jesus Christ: The Hermeneutical Bases of Dogmatic Theology*. Eugene, OR: Wipf & Stock, 1997.

Fuller, Daniel. *Easter Faith and History*. Grand Rapids: Eerdmans, 1965.

Fuller, Reginald H. *The Formation of the Resurrection Narratives*. New York: Macmillan, 1971.

Gerhardsson, Birger. *Memory and Manuscript: Oral Tradition and Written Transmission in Rabbinic Judaism and Early Christianity*. Uppsala, Sweden: Gleerup, 1961.

Gilkey, Langdon. *Reaping the Whirlwind: A Christian Interpretation of History*. New York: Seabury, 1976.

Gillis, Martha Schull. "Resurrecting the Atonement." In *Feminist and Womanist Essays in Reformed Dogmatics*, edited by Amy Platinga Pauw and Serene Jones, 125–38. Louisville: Westminster John Knox, 2006.

Godzieba, Anthony, et al. "Resurrection—Interruption—Transformation: Incarnation as Hermeneutical Strategy." *Theological Studies* 67 (2006) 777–815.

Grenz, Stanley J. *A Primer on Postmodernism*. Grand Rapids: Eerdmans, 1996.

Habermas, Gary R. *Ancient Evidence for the Life of Jesus: Historical Records of His Death and Resurrection*. New York: Thomas Nelson, 1984.

Hall, Douglas John. *The Cross in Our Context: Jesus and the Suffering World*. Minneapolis: Fortress, 2003.

Hardy, Richard. "The Resurrection: Keystone of Third World Spirituality." *Grail* 3 (1987) 96–105.

Harvey, A. E. *Jesus and the Constraints of History*. Philadelphia: Westminster, 1982.

Harvey, Van Austin. *The Historian and the Believer: The Morality of Historical Knowledge and Christian Belief*. New York: Macmillan, 1968.

Haught, John F. *God after Darwin: A Theology of Evolution*. Boulder, CO: Westview, 2000.

Hebblethwaite, Brian. "The Resurrection and the Incarnation." In *The Resurrection of Jesus Christ*, edited by Paul Avis, 155–70. London: Darton, Longman & Todd, 1993.

Henaut, W. Barry. "Is the 'Historical Jesus' a Theological Construct?" In Arnal and Desjardins, *Whose Historical Jesus?*, 241–68.

Hengel, Martin. *The Four Gospels and the One Gospel of Jesus Christ*. Harrisburg, PA: Trinity, 2000.

Higton, Mike. *Christ, Providence, and History: Hans W. Frei's Public Theology*. New York: T. & T. Clark, 2004.

Bibliography

Hooke, S. H. *The Resurrection of Christ as History and Experience*. London: Darton, Longman & Todd, 1967.
House, Adrian. *Francis of Assisi: A Revolutionary Life*. Mahwah, NJ: HiddenSpring, 2001.
Jenson, Robert W. "Once More: The Jesus of History and the Christ of Faith." *Dialog* 11 (1972) 118–24.
Jeremias, Joachim. *The Problem of the Historical Jesus*. Philadelphia: Fortress, 1964.
Johnson, John J. "Hans Frei as Unlikely Apologist for the Historicity of the Resurrection." *Evangelical Quarterly* 76 (2004) 135–51.
Johnson, Luke Timothy. *The Real Jesus: The Misguided Quest for the Historical Jesus and the Truth of the Historical Gospels*. San Francisco: HarperSanFrancisco, 1996.
Kähler, Martin. *The So-Called Historical Jesus and the Historic Biblical Christ*. Philadelphia: Fortress, 1964.
Käsemann, Ernst. *Essays on New Testament Themes*. Philadelphia: Fortress, 1964.
Keating, James F. "Epistemology and the Theological Application of Jesus Research." In *Christology: Memory, Inquiry, Practice*, edited by Anne M. Clifford and Anthony J. Godzieba, 18–43. Maryknoll: Orbis, 2003.
Kloppenborg, John S. *Excavating Q: The History and Setting of the Sayings Gospel*. Minneapolis: Fortress, 2000.
———. *The Formation of Q: Trajectories in Ancient Wisdom Collections*. Philadelphia: Fortress, 1987.
———. *Q Parallels: Synopsis, Critical Notes, and Concordance*. Sonoma, CA: Polebridge, 1988.
Krell, David Ferrell, ed. *Martin Heidegger: Basic Writings*. San Francisco: HarperSanFrancisco, 1977.
Ladd, George Eldon. "Resurrection and History." *Dialog* 1 (1962) 55–56.
Lapide, Pinchas. *The Resurrection of Jesus: A Jewish Perspective*. Minneapolis: Augsburg, 1983.
Levine, Amy-Jill. *The Misunderstood Jew: The Church and the Scandal of the Jewish Jesus*. San Francisco: HarperSanFrancisco, 2006.
———. *The Social and Ethnic Dimenions of Matthean Salvation History*. Lewiston, NY: Mellen, 1988.
———, ed. *Women Like This: New Perspectives on Jewish Women in the Greco-Roman World*. Ann Arbor, MI: Scholars, 1991.
Libânio, João Batista. "Hope, Utopia, Resurrection." In *Systematic Theology: Perspectives from Liberation Theology*, edited by Jon Sobrino and Ignacio Ellacuria, 279–90. Maryknoll: Orbis, 1993.
Lincoln, Andrew T., and Angus Paddison, eds. *Christology and Scripture: Interdisciplinary Perspectives*. London: T. & T. Clark, 2007.
Lindbeck, George. "Barth and Textuality." *Theology Today* 43 (1986) 361–75.
———. *The Nature of Doctrine: Religion and Theology in a Postliberal Age*. Louisville: Westminster John Knox, 1984.
Lowder, Jeffrey Jay. "Historical Evidence and the Empty Tomb Story: A Reply to William Lane Craig." In *The Empty Tomb: Jesus Beyond the Grave*, edited by Robert M. Price and Jeffrey Jay Lowder, 261–306. New York: Prometheus, 2005.
Lüdemann, Gerd. *The Resurrection of Jesus: History, Experience, and Theology*. Minneapolis: Fortress, 1994.
Mack, Burton. *The Lost Gospel: The Book Q and Christian Origins*. Minneapolis: Fortress, 1988.

Bibliography

Macleod, Donald. "The Christology of Wolfhart Pannenberg." *Themelios* 25 (2000) 19–41.
MacQuarrie, John. *Twentieth-Century Religious Thought*. Harrisburg, PA: Trinity, 2002.
Mahoney, Jack. *Christianity in Evolution: An Exploration*. Washington, DC: Georgetown University Press, 2011.
Martin, Michael. "The Resurrection as Initially Improbable." In *The Empty Tomb: Jesus Beyond the Grave*, edited by Robert M. Price and Jeffrey Jay Lowder, 43–54. New York: Prometheus, 2005.
Marxsen, Willi. *The Resurrection of Jesus of Nazareth*. London: SCM, 1970.
Matera, Frank J. *New Testament Christology*. Louisville: Westminster John Knox, 1999.
McFague, Sally. *Models of God: Theology for an Ecological, Nuclear Age*. Philadelphia: Fortress, 1987.
McGilchrist, Iain. *The Master and His Emissary: The Divided Brain and the Making of the Western World*. New Haven: Yale University Press, 2009.
McGrath, Alister E. *The Genesis of Doctrine: A Study in the Foundation of Doctrinal Criticism*. Vancouver: Regent College Publishing, 1990.
McIntire, C. T. "Historical Study and the Historical Dimension of Our World." In *History and Historical Understanding*, edited by C. T. McIntire and Ronald Wells, 17–40. Grand Rapids: Eerdmans, 1984.
McKnight, Edgar V. *Jesus Christ in History and Scripture: A Poetic and Sectarian Perspective*. Macon, GA: Mercer, 1999.
McKnight, Scot. *Jesus and His Death: Historiography, the Historical Jesus, and Atonement Theory*. Waco, TX: Baylor University Press, 2005.
McNeill, John T., ed. *The Institutes of Religion*. Philadelphia: Westminster, 1960.
Meier, John P. *A Marginal Jew: Rethinking the Historical Jesus*. Vol. 1, *The Roots of the Problem and the Person*. New York: Doubleday, 1994.
Meyer, Ben F. *The Aims of Jesus*. London: SCM, 1979.
———. *Critical Realism and the New Testament*. Allison Park, PA: Pickwick, 1989.
———. *Reality and Illusion in New Testament Scholarship: A Primer in Critical Realist Hermeneutics*. Collegeville: Liturgical, 1994.
Michalson, Gordon E. "Pannenberg on the Resurrection and Historical Method." *Scottish Journal of Theology* 33 (1980) 345–59.
Moltmann, Jürgen. *God in Creation*. Minneapolis: Fortress, 1993.
———. *History and the Triune God*. New York: Crossroad, 1992.
———. "The Resurrection of Christ: Hope for the World." In D'Costa, *Resurrection Reconsidered*, 73–86.
———. *Theology of Hope: On the Ground and the Implications of a Christian Eschatology*. Minneapolis: Fortress, 1993.
———. *The Way of Jesus Christ*. Minneapolis: Fortress, 1993.
Momigliano, Arnoldo. *The Classical Foundations of Modern Historiography*. Los Angeles: University of California Press, 1990.
Morgan, Robert. "James Dunn's Jesus Remembered." *Expository Times* 116 (2004) 1–6.
Moxnes, Halvor. "The Theological Importance of the 'Third Quest' for the Historical Jesus." In Arnal and Desjardins, *Whose Historical Jesus?*, 132–42.
Neill, Stephen, and N. T. Wright. *The Interpretation of the New Testament, 1861–1986*. New York: Oxford University Press, 1988.
Newbiggin, Lesslie. *The Gospel in a Pluralistic Society*. Grand Rapids, MI: William B Eerdmans Publishing Company, 1989.

Newman, Carey C. "Resurrection as Re-embodiment: N. T. Wright's Resurrection of the Son of God." *Expository Times* 116 (2005) 228–33.
Niebuhr, H. Richard. *The Meaning of Revelation*. New York: Macmillan, 1946.
Niebuhr, Richard R. *Resurrection and Historical Reason: A Study of Theological Method*. New York: Scribner, 1957.
Oberdorfer, Bernd. "Schleiermacher on Eschatology and Resurrection." In *Resurrection: Theological and Scientific Assessments*, edited by Ted Peters et al., 165–82. Grand Rapids: Eerdmans, 2002.
O'Collins, Gerald. "Is the Resurrection an 'Historical Event'?" In *The Historical Jesus: Critical Concepts in Religious Studies*, edited by Craig A. Evans, 317–23. New York: Routledge, 2004.
———. *Jesus Risen: An Historical, Fundamental and Systematic Examination of Christ's Resurrection*. New York: Paulist, 1987.
———. *Jesus Risen: The Resurrection—What Actually Happened and What Does It Mean?* London: Darton, Longman & Todd, 1987.
———. "The Resurrection: The State of the Questions." In *The Resurrection: An Interdisciplinary Symposium on the Resurrection of Jesus*, edited by Stephen T. Davis et al., 5–40. New York: Oxford University Press, 1997.
Ogden, Schubert. *New Testament and Theology*. Philadelphia: Fortress, 1984.
O'Hanlon, Gerard F. *The Immutability of God in the Theology of Hans Urs von Balthasar*. New York: Cambridge University Press, 1990.
Olson, Roger E. "Back to the Bible (Almost): Why Yale's Postliberal Theologians Deserve an Evangelical Hearing." *Christianity Today*, May 20, 1996.
Ott, Heinrich. "The Historical Jesus and the Ontology of History." In Braaten and Harrisville, *The Historical Jesus and the Kerygmatic Christ*, 142–71.
Padgett, Allan G. "Advice for Religious Historians: On the Myth of the Purely Historical Jesus." In *The Resurrection: An Interdisciplinary Symposium on the Resurrection of Jesus*, edited by Stephen T. Davis et al., 287–307. New York: Oxford University Press, 1997.
Pannenberg, Wolfhart. "Dogmatic Theses on the Doctrine of Revelation." In *Revelation as History*, 125–58. New York: Macmillan, 1968.
———. "Hermeneutics and Universal History." In *History and Hermeneutic*, edited by Robert Funk, 122–52. New York: Harper & Row, 1967.
———. "History and the Reality of the Resurrection." In D'Costa, *Resurrection Reconsidered*, 319–26.
———. *Jesus—God and Man*. Philadelphia: Westminster, 1974.
———. "The Resurrection of Jesus: History and Theology." *Dialog* 38 (1999) 20–25.
Pecknold, C. C. *Transforming Postliberal Theology: George Lindbeck, Pragmatism, and Scripture*. New York: T. & T. Clark, 2005.
Perkins, Pheme. *Resurrection: New Testament Witness and Contemporary Reflection*. Garden City: Doubleday, 1984.
Peters, Ted. "Resurrection: The Conceptual Challenge." In *Resurrection: Theological and Scientific Assessments*, edited by Ted Peters et al., 297–321. Grand Rapids: Eerdmans, 2002.
———. "Shorter Communications: The Use of Analogy in Historical Method." *Catholic Biblical Quarterly* 35 (1973) 475–84.
Phillips, Timothy R., and Dennis L. Okholm, eds. *The Nature of Confession: Evangelicals & Postliberals in Conversation*. Downers Grove: InterVarsity, 1996.

Bibliography

Placher, William C. *The Domestication of Transcendence: How Modern Thinking about God Went Wrong.* Louisville: Westminster John Knox, 1996.

———. *The Triune God: An Essay in Postliberal Theology.* Louisville: Westminster John Knox, 2007.

Polkinghorne, John. *Science and Theology: An Introduction.* Minneapolis: Fortress, 1998.

Popper, Karl R. *The Poverty of Historicism.* London: Routledge & Paul, 1961.

Powell, Mark Allen. *Jesus as a Figure in History: How Modern Historians View the Man from Galilee.* Louisville: Westminster John Knox, 1998.

Quash, Ben. *Theology and the Drama of History.* Cambridge: Cambridge University Press, 2005.

Ratzinger, Joseph. *Jesus of Nazareth: From the Baptism in the Jordan to the Transfiguration.* Toronto: Doubleday, 2007.

Renan, Ernest. *The Life of Jesus.* New York: Modern Library, 1927.

Richardson, Alan. "Resurrection of Jesus Christ." *Theology* 74 (1971) 146–54.

Roberts, Alexander, and James Donaldson, eds. *The Ante-Nicene Fathers.* 10 vols. Grand Rapids: Eerdmans, 1885.

Robinson, James M. *A New Quest of the Historical Jesus.* Naperville, IL: Allenson, 1959.

Russell, John Robert. "Bodily Resurrection, Eschatology, and Scientific Cosmology." In *Resurrection: Theological and Scientific Assessments*, edited by Ted Peters et al., 3–30. Grand Rapids: Eerdmans, 2002.

Santayana, George. *The Life of Reason.* Vol. 1. New York: Scribner, 1928.

Schaff, Philip, ed. *A Select Library of Nicene and Post-Nicene Fathers of the Christian Church.* 1st series. 14 vols. Grand Rapids: Eerdmans, 1886.

Schaff, Philip, and Henry Wace, eds. *A Select Library of Nicene and Post-Nicene Fathers of the Christian Church.* 2nd series. 14 vols. Grand Rapids: Eerdmans, 1891.

Schmidt, Lawrence Edward. "Historical Process and Hermeneutical Method in the Theologies of John Macquarrie, Schubert Ogden, and Wolfhart Pannenberg." PhD diss., St. Michael's College, University of Toronto, 1985.

Schmidt, Peter. "The Interpretation of the Resurrection: Historical and Theological Truth." *Communio* 11 (1984) 75–88.

Schnelle, Udo. *Theology of the New Testament.* Grand Rapids: Baker Academic, 2009.

Schüssler Fiorenza, Elisabeth. *Jesus: Miriam's Child, Sophia's Prophet; Critical Issues in Feminist Christology.* New York: Continuum, 1995.

Schüssler Fiorenza, Francis. *Foundational Theology: Jesus and the Church.* New York: Crossroad, 1984.

———. "The Resurrection of Jesus and Roman Catholic Theology." In *The Resurrection: An Interdisciplinary Symposium on the Resurrection of Jesus*, edited by Stephen T. Davis et al., 213–48. New York: Oxford University Press, 1997.

Schweitzer, Albert. *The Quest of the Historical Jesus: A Critical Study of Its Progress from Reimarus to Wrede.* New York: Macmillan, 1910.

Sherwin-White, A. N. *Roman Society and Roman Law in the New Testament.* Oxford: Clarendon, 1963.

Shils, Edward A., and Henry A. Finch. *Max Weber on the Meaning of the Social Sciences: Collected Essays.* Glencoe, IL: Free Press, 1949.

Shuster, Marguerite. "The Preaching of the Resurrection of Christ in Augustine, Luther, Barth, and Thielicke." In *The Resurrection: An Interdisciplinary Symposium on the Resurrection of Jesus*, edited by Stephen T. Davis et al., 308–38. New York: Oxford University Press, 1997.

Bibliography

Spence, Brian John. *Von Balthasar and Moltmann: Two Responses to Hegel on the Subject of the Incarnation and the Death of God*. ThD diss., Regis College, Toronto, 1996.
Staudinger, Hugo. "The Resurrection of Jesus Christ as Saving Event and as 'Object' of Historical Research." *Scottish Journal of Theology* 36 (1983) 309–26.
Stewart, Robert B., ed. *The Resurrection of Jesus: John Dominic Crossan and N. T. Wright in Dialogue*. Minneapolis: Fortress, 2006.
Strauss, David Friedrich. *The Life of Jesus Critically Examined*. Philadelphia: Fortress, 1972.
Swinburne, Richard. *The Resurrection of God Incarnate*. Oxford: Clarendon, 2003.
Tang, Siu-Kwong. *God's History in the Theology of Jürgen Moltmann*. Bern: Lang, 1996.
Taylor, Charles. *A Secular Age*. Cambridge: Harvard University Press, 2007.
Taylor, Vincent. *The Formation of the Gospel Tradition*. London: Macmillan, 1935.
Tilley, Terrence W. *History, Theology, and Faith: Dissolving the Modern Problematic*. Maryknoll: Orbis, 2004.
———. *Postmodern Theologies: The Challenge of Religious Diversity*. Maryknoll: Orbis, 1995.
Torrance, Thomas F. *Space, Time, and Resurrection*. Edinburgh: Handsel, 1976.
Tosh, John. *The Pursuit of History: Aims, Methods, and New Directions in the Study of Modern History*. 4th ed. London: Longmans, 2006.
Troeltsch, Ernst. *The Christian Religion*. Minneapolis: Augsburg Fortress, 1991.
———. *Religion in History*. Edinburgh: T. & T. Clark, 1991.
Tuckett, Christopher. *Christology and the New Testament*. Louisville: Westminster John Knox, 2001.
Vansina, Jan. *Oral Tradition as History*. Madison, WI: University of Wisconsin Press, 1985.
Vedder, Ben. *Heidegger's Philosophy of Religion: From God to the Gods*. Pittsburgh: Duquesne University Press, 2007.
Vermes, Geza. *The Resurrection*. New York: Doubleday, 2008.
Vidu, Adonis. *Postliberal Theological Method*. Eugene, OR: Wipf & Stock, 2007.
Watson, Francis. "Is the Historian Competent to Speak of the Resurrection of Jesus? A Study in Hermeneutics." *Kerygma und Dogma* 55 (2009) 52–72.
Webster, John. "Resurrection and Scripture." In *Christology and Scripture: Interdisciplinary Perspectives*, edited by Andrew T. Lincoln and Angus Paddison, 138–55. New York: T. & T. Clark, 2008.
Weibe, Ben. "Interpretation and Historical Criticism: Jürgen Moltmann." *Restoration Quarterly* 24 (1981) 155–66.
Westerholm, Stephen. "The Christ of Faith: Context." In Arnal and Desjardins, *Whose Historical Jesus?*, 238–40.
White, Hayden. *The Content of the Form: Narrative Discourse in Historical Representation*. Baltimore: Johns Hopkins University, 1987.
Wilckens, Ulrich. *Resurrection: Biblical Testimony to the Resurrection; An Historical Examination and Explanation*. Atlanta: John Knox, 1978.
Williams, John R. "Heidegger and the Theologians." *Heythrop Journal* 12 (1971) 258–80.
Wood, Laurence W. "History and Hermeneutics: A Pannenbergian Perspective." *Wesleyan Theological Journal* 16 (1981) 7–22.
World Council of Churches. "God in Nature and History." In *God, History, and Historians: An Anthology of Modern Christian Views of History*, edited by C. T. McIntire, 291–328. New York: Oxford University Press, 1977.

Bibliography

Wright, N.T. "Christian Origins and the Resurrection of Jesus: The Resurrection of Jesus as a Historical Problem." *Sewanee Theological Review* 41 (1998) 107–23.
———. *Jesus and the Victory of God*. Minneapolis: Fortress, 1996.
———. *The New Testament and the People of God*. Minneapolis: Fortress, 1992.
———. *The Resurrection of the Son of God*. Minneapolis: Fortress, 2003.
Yarchin, William. *History of Biblical Interpretation: A Reader*. Peabody, MA: Hendrickson, 2004.

Index

Appleby, Joyce, 46
Aquinas, Thomas, 28–29
Athanasius, 27–28
Augustine, 28
Bacon, Francis, 39
Barth, Karl, vii, 58–59, 125
Barthes, Roland, 44
Bauckham, Richard, 104
Bayle, Pierre, 39
Bloch, Marc, 41
Boeve, Lieven, 128–129, 131
Borg, Marcus, 87, 89–90
Bray, Gerald, 72n2
Breisach, Ernst, 35–39, 50
Brown, Raymond E., 126, 127
Bultmann, Rudolf, vii, 57–58, 79, 110
Burridge, R. A., 36–37, 50
Calvin, Jean, 29
Carnley, Peter, 97–99
Carr, Edward Hallett, 41
Cavin, Robert Greg, 65
Cicero, 36
Clark, Elizabeth, 43–49
Coakley, Sarah, 68
Cochrane, Eric, 48
Collingwood, R.G., 40–41
Cone, James H., 131–33
Cönzelmann, Hans, 59
Craffert, Pieter F., 101–2, 104
Craig, William Lane, 66, 75–76, 89
Crenshaw, James L., 108
Crossan, John Dominic, vii, 79–81, 84, 86, 89

Derrida, Jacques, 44n29
Droysen, Johann Gustav, 40
Dufour, Xavier Leon, 99
Elton, G.R., 41–42
Evans, Craig A., 81n26
Fergusson, David A., 100
Foucault, Michel, 43n24, 45
Frei, Hans, 104–7, 110–11
Gerhardsson, Birger, 37n7
Godzieba, Anthony, 127–9, 131
Habermas, Gary R., 76, 89, 94
Harvey, Van Austin, 59
Haught, John F., 130–1
Hegel, G.F., 135
Heidegger, 58
Higton, Mike, 105, 106
House, Adrian, 38n29
Hughes, Gerard J., 134
Hume, David, 39, 64–65
Hunt, Lynn, 46
Ignatius, 27, 37
Irenaeus, 37
Jacob, Margaret, 46
Jeremias, Joachim, 59
Käsemann, Ernst, 59, 73, 83
Kähler, Martin, 57–58
Lapide, Pinchas, viii, 78–79, 89
Levine, Amy-Jill, 83–83, 89
Libânio, João Batista, 133
Lüdemann, Gerd, 81–82, 84, 89, 96
Luther, Martin, 39
Mack, Burton, 73
Mahoney, Jack, 134n23

151

Index

Martin, Michael, 64
Marxsen, Willi, 82–83, 84, 89, 94, 97
McGilchrist, Iain, 125n3, 137–8
McIntire, C. T., 47–48, 51, 96
McKnight, Scot, 111
Meier, John, 85–6, 89–90, 94, 100
Meyer, Ben F., 84, 96, 107
Moltmann, Jürgen, vii, 60, 61–62, 68
Momigliano, Arnoldo, 36, 50
Niebuhr, H. Richard, 59
O'Collins, Gerald, 99–100
Ogden, Schubert, 58n7
Origen, 27
Ott, Heinrich, 59
Padgett, Allan G., 93–96, 102
Pannenberg, Wolfhart, 59–61, 62, 64, 68, 88, 132
Perkins, Pheme, 77–78, 89
Peters, Ted, 61
Placher, William C., 3, 135
Polkinghorne, John, 65
Popper, Karl R., 41
Powell, Mark Allen, 74, 81n26
Ratzinger, Joseph, 135n27, 139
Renan, Ernest, 72
Robinson, James M., 73, 86

Santayana, George, 45
Saracino, Michele, 129–31
Schleiermacher, Friedrich, 72
Schmidt, Peter, 99–100
Schnelle, Udo, 50–51, 87–88, 89–90
Schüssler-Fiorenza, 137
Schüssler Fiorenza, Francis, 102–3, 104, 110
Schweitzer, Albert, 72–73
Strauss, David Friedrich, 72, 79
Swinburne, Richard, 64–65, 76, 110
Taylor, Charles, 119
Tertullian, 27
Thucydides, 36
Tilley, Terrence W., 39n12, 59n11, 66–67, 100
Troeltsch, Ernst, 54–57, 58, 60, 61, 64
Vansina, Jan, 37
Vermes, Geza, 65–66
Voltaire, 39
von Balthasar, Hans Urs, vii, 60, 63–64, 68, 86, 135–6
White, Hayden, 42–43, 51
Whitehead, Alfred North, 114
Wright, N.T., vii, 26n3, 84–85, 86, 89–90, 107–10

www.ingramcontent.com/pod-product-compliance
Lightning Source LLC
Chambersburg PA
CBHW051107160426
43193CB00010B/1347